QUIET PLACES

QUIET PLACES

JANE RUBIETTA

BETHANY HOUSE PUBLISHERS
MINNEAPOLIS, MINNESOTA 55438

Quiet Places
Copyright © 1997
Jane A. Rubietta

Cover design by Eric Walljasper

Published by Bethany House Publishers
A Ministry of Bethany Fellowship International
11300 Hampshire Avenue South
Minneapolis, Minnesota 55438

Printed in the United States of America by
Bethany Press International, Minneapolis, Minnesota 55438

Library of Congress Cataloging-in-Publication Data
Rubietta, Jane A.
   Quiet places: a woman's guide to personal retreat / by Jane A. Rubietta.
     p. cm.
   ISBN 0–7642–2001–2
   1. Women—Religious life. 2. Retreats. 3. Spiritual life—Christianity. I. Title.
BV4527.R82   1997
248.8'43—dc21   97–33849
                                                    CIP

To my husband, Rich, a musician,
who urged me to listen to the song in my soul;
And to my God, who leads me into quiet places.

JANE A. RUBIETTA has a marketing and management degree from Indiana University and has worked toward her Master's at Trinity Divinity School.

Conducting women's seminars, she discovered a large percentage of the women who attended desired a practical how-to guide for personal retreat. *Quiet Places* builds on her popular writing for *Today's Christian Woman*, *Virtue*, *Marriage Partnership*, *Christian Reader*, and *Christianity Today*. Jane's husband, Rich, is a pastor. They have three children and make their home in Grayslake, Illinois.

Acknowledgments

For their help in making *Quiet Places* a reality, I thank God for:

My critique group: Lynn Austin, Joy Heimann, Cleo Lampos, and Pam Simpson, who kept me to my calling;

My covenant group: Linda Adams, Adele Calhoun, Karen Mains, Linda Richardson, Marilyn Stewart, and Sibyl Towner, who faithfully sheltered me with their umbrella of protection and love;

My parents, who gave me the gift of books and a love for words, and by their strength encouraged me to dream;

My parents-in-law, Jim and Marie, who gladly provided their home and their support so that I could write uninterrupted;

Mom and Dad Whiz, who have prayed for me every day for fifteen years;

Steve Laube, whose wisdom and insight make him a good editor, and whose kindness and laughter make him a good friend;

Beth Elliott, a dear friend and spiritual mentor before such terms were popular; and Kathy Fairbairn and Ellen Binder, who have linked hands with me on this soul-journey;

My husband, Rich, and our precious children, Ruthie, Zak, and Josh, who daily tutor me in real Christianity.

Contents

And Jesus said,
"Come with Me by yourselves to a quiet place
and get some rest."

Mark 6:31, NIV

Preface

Fog swirled, swallowing the car in front of me. Dense, impenetrable, the wall of white threw my lights back into my eyes. I crept along the country roads, visibility less than an eighth of a mile. One headlight veered crazily into the pavement, like a drunken watchman; the other pointed bravely ahead into the whitewashed night.

In weather like this, mountain drivers pray for a front car, for taillights to guide them through the fog like a rope strung between barns in a blizzard. Fogs I'm familiar with. They obscured the mountain roads of my childhood, blinded me on the Pennsylvania Turnpike, and frequently close in on my spirit and soul in the form of depression. This evening, fifty miles west of Chicago, no taillights pulled me; no front car cut a swath. The only guides were the white strip on one side of the road and the reflectors protruding from the center line.

The road worsened; fog spread out in a blanket over the flat farmland. The crawling pace magnified every rut, until I almost felt my way to the driveway of the retreat house. The welcoming light over the door wavered in the whiteness. Shaka, our Siberian husky, whined and thumped her tail, sensing our destination at hand.

Inside, the fireplace yawned a blank welcome. Ironic, I thought, unloading meager provisions and crumpling papers for a fire: fitting that the fog accompanied me on this journey to the center of the soul, this personal retreat. Telling that my only escorts were crazy, mismatched headlights and the lines on the road.

For this has been the story of my life. At thirty-six, with a pastor-husband and three elementary-age children, the fog simply disguises itself: as busyness, as self-importance, as lack of confidence, as false security. Too often, rather than the guides written in lines in my soul, my markers have been what other people did or did not do; what other women didn't seem to need; or what someone, somewhere, defined as normal.

Inching along the road of spiritual self-care, I have ended up writing and speaking to women in fogs of similar density. When I speak about personal retreats, they clutch their tattered robes of exhaustion around themselves and stand in line to ask questions. The concept is so foreign to their independent, forge-ahead spirits that they cannot comprehend a starting place. *Quiet Places* is for us. For the valiant woman juggling jobs, relationships, hearth, home, and church, who can no longer afford to neglect the keening of her heart within her breast. If the fog does not lift, may we at least have some lines and reflectors put down along the road to guide us.

Introduction: How to Use This Book

In *Quiet Places*, each chapter can be used either as an individual retreat or on a devotional basis. With its unique format, *Quiet Places* also works in a small group setting, on a getaway with other women, or in a Sunday school class. Each of the twelve chapters stands alone, and contains suggestions for filling the unaccustomed time spent in the presence of God by ourselves. Whether retreating from the busyness at the dining-room table or getting away for a larger block of time, we want to follow the Spirit's leading when experiencing an individual retreat. So these are truly only suggestions, thought-provokers, spirit-prodders.

Initially, the retreat format may be uncomfortable. As much as my soul yearns for the green, quiet hills of Psalm 23, on arrival I may feel simply aimless and weary, a traveler descending upon her destination too tired to focus, too empty to pray, too cluttered to think.

Emphasizing a certain subject, reading relevant quotes, and directing the mind to Scriptures that are attuned to the given topic all help to maximize the precious time spent alone with our God. Each chapter offers possibilities for soul-care, either in small bites or in larger chunks of time:

- Reading for Reflection
- Quotes for Contemplation
- Scriptures for Meditation
- Journaling
- Prayers of Confession, Praise, Petition
- Moments for Creation

- Silence
- Questions for Reflection
- Hymn of Praise

Reading for Reflection

Each chapter begins with a warm-up, an opening stretch, and an introduction to the retreat topic. Many of these rose from my own encounters, from observing life on the soul side and on the outside.

Quotes for Contemplation

A brilliant beam of sunlight streams through the leaded glass, painting prisms on the far wall. The neighbor's house catches the last of the sunlight on her windows and bounces it into my front room. We profit twice from her reflected light.

When on a personal retreat, we can also use reflected light. On my desk at home are classics by Anne Morrow Lindbergh, Annie Dillard, Henri Nouwen, and George MacDonald, to name only a few. If I can't sit at their feet literally and absorb the light they share, then they can shine the light of Christ to me through the printed page. Here are the mentors, people who have pressed forward into the Light of Jesus. These real-life people challenge the soul, make me question my assumptions, call me higher in all my relationships. These friends are beacons in storm-tossed nights, illuminating the rocks and ledges.

Quotes from well-known (and not so well-known) authors are included in *Quiet Places*. Here we benefit from another's exploration of green pastures and still spaces; their footsteps guide us to healing places, provoke our thoughts, prod our spirits. In a world desperately lacking visible mentors, these become our soul-models.

Scriptures for Meditation

One of the surest ways to be thoroughly in God's presence is through His Word. While the Lord speaks to us in a variety of ways, Scripture rings a bell through our souls, clearly calling us to God. Although I try to bathe my soul in Scripture every day, sometimes it's more like a sponge bath. A personal retreat provides time to meditate, to search out a particular subject, to read until the shadowed corners of the heart fill with light.

The selected Scriptures may be familiar; all are related to the retreat topic. You may want to choose one and begin to memorize it, or compare it in different versions.

When our spirits are weak and emaciated from a deprivation diet, the Scriptures feed us and fill us, quenching our thirst but at the same time making us thirstier still. O to sing with the prophet Jeremiah, "Thy words were found and I ate them, and Thy words became for me a joy and the delight of my heart" (15:16).

A favorite retreat version of Scripture is Eugene H. Peterson's *The Message*. He renders Psalm 119:105, "By your words I can see where I'm going; they throw a beam of light on my dark path."

Allow that beam of light to pour over you as you luxuriate in its glowing warmth. Take time to soak up each verse, meditating on it, journaling about it, free-flowing between confession and praise and petition. Let His words fill you, freeing your heart to dance out of the dark like airport searchlights circling a night sky. Agendas aren't necessary for this time in the Light; free the Word and the Spirit to highlight important things.

Journaling

There are no rules for the journaling time; here we scrape all the bugs off the windshield to better see the Light. In the journal we dump the accumulated soul-toxins. The clean white pages of the notebook become a metaphor for Jesus, pure and sinless, receiving our spots and splatters and wiping the windshield clean.

Sometimes journaling is a waterfall of words, when all the anxieties and angers and aggravations pour out. At other times, think back to conversations, attitudes, and relationships and bring them into the Light. Regardless of how we use a journal, it can be an instrument for confession, a place to leave the uglies at the foot of the cross.

Here, too, is a quiet place to think in ink about Scripture; seeing the Word in our own writing sometimes highlights the Spirit's message to us. If your soul quickens over a particular passage or phrase, write it in your journal and catch the feelings as they spread.

Through journaling, we can track the Spirit's work in our lives. The journal cements our footprints along this road to personal holiness.

Prayers

Confession

Jose delivers pizza. Once he stopped by our house with some dough the company was throwing out because a new shipment had come. The dough was fresh and moist, perfect for baking. We crowded around him, delighted, envisioning twenty pizzas bubbling from the oven and warming our table.

But I became busy, forgetting the little clumps of dough cooling in the spare refrigerator. Several days later, I found the door ajar. "Who left this open?" I bellowed into the house. Evidently, the door burst open because of the forgotten dough, which had expanded its cardboard boundaries and filled the entire refrigerator.

Unconfessed sin is like that expanding dough. Eventually, it tears open our souls and causes spoilage. We cannot afford such waste.

Confession can be one of the most difficult, painstaking stages of the soul-journey. Regular journaling makes confession easier, but all that writing becomes grueling. Still, with unconfessed sin a stowaway in the corners of the heart, we are rendered ineffectual.

"Search me, O God, and know my heart; try me and know my anxious thoughts. And see if there be any hurtful way in me, and lead me in the everlasting way," sings the psalmist (Ps. 139:23). This Scripture can open prayer time. In the silence that follows, blemishes erupt from deep within: forgotten incidents, conversations where the tongue whipped into action before the mind seized control. Times when we ignored, or failed to love, or loathed in the hidden recesses of the heart. In the stillness following confession, God's forgiveness washes our souls clean. Praise is a natural response to the glorious freedom of forgiveness.

Praise

Affirmation is vital in intimate relationships, and none more so than in our relationship with the Lord. The Scriptures call forth praise from the people for the person of God.

Setting aside time during a retreat to enjoy the created world is a thrilling way to affirm God. On one getaway, I slipped off to a monastery. Autumn beamed and beckoned from the perimeters of lovely green fields. Calling this a "Praise and Thanksgiving Walk," my thoughts turned to observe the Lord's handiwork. A nest in a bristle bush, a perfectly shaped pinecone, the baby-blanket softness of a grassy area: all these loosed my tongue to praise Him.

God could have made the world merely functional. But He chose instead to create loveliness, sharing this incredible beauty with each observer. Shivers chased up my spine as I looked down a grass-covered road, rarely used. An aura of yellow shone from a maple, and the closer I came the greater my love for God pounded in my heart. Such an amber light surrounded the tree that I wondered if the temple glowed as radiantly when the Shekinah glory rested there.

Scripture tells us God inhabits the praises of His people, and our praise becomes a fragrant aroma, a love offering, an anointing of oil from the flasks of our lives.

Petition

Prayers of petition come the easiest to most people. Bringing a list of needs into God's throne room is more natural than setting aside our own desires to praise Him. But Scripture is clear that we are to ask, seek, knock, ever the importunate widow banging on the door until her request is granted.

Though I am by no means a prayer warrior, most of my prayer life has been weighted in the petition area. Lists, pictures, and other gimmicks remind me to pray. But it's easy in the routine of prayer lists to forget to follow the Spirit's leading. Try praying the great prayers of Scripture— Jesus' prayer in the Garden (John 17), Paul's petition for the church in Ephesus (Eph. 1:17ff)—when calling to mind the names of loved ones. At other times, envision the people on the list and imagine them in your hand, offering each up in silence before the Lord.

Silence

Of all the components of healthy soul-care, none is quite so alien to our loud, frenzied, talkative lifestyle as silence. By nature, we are relational people who rely more on our own words to relate to one another than on the other person's.

The antithesis of the babbling, child-on-Santa's-lap type of praying to which many of us resort, being silent in the presence of God is called *contemplative prayer.*

The operative word is *practice.* Thoughts constantly interrupt, intruders in this hesitant process. To get started, follow some advice from contemplatives: begin with a phrase from Scripture, such as "The Lord is my Shepherd," or with a brief prayer, "Christ have mercy." This helps clear the mind's monitor, becomes a hedge barring intrusive thoughts. Brother Lawrence called this lifting of oneself into the presence of God "holy inactivity."

Perhaps this holy stillness will last only seconds before running thoughts spill over and escape. But those seconds in silence! In this quiet place, there is a sense of entering into eternity. An opening is made with the King of the universe; an audience granted. Peter's words echo, "With the Lord one day is as a thousand years, and a thousand years as one day," (2 Pet. 3:8), and a taste of heaven touches the palates of our spirits. A veil is pulled aside, opening to His presence.

At times, through the silence, clear direction from the Lord may emerge in regard to a decision spread before Him. More than anything, though, His love will line the heart's walls. He embraces and empowers through silence.

One commentator writes, "All [of Jesus'] words were born in silence: they came from those mountain prayers in which he met with God face-to-face. All his power came from silence: 'Be still, and know that I am God.' "[1]

In the silence comes the knowing.

Questions for Reflection

This section offers a few questions designed to help each seeker further investigate the subject of the chapter; questions no one else asks, questions we might not ask ourselves, questions a loving mentor might investigate with us. It may take a lifetime to resolve some of these questions, but in the safety of God's presence we begin to probe.

We live in a society without focus, a tangential world where conversations begin one place and end miles away, totally off track, topic abandoned, target forgotten, question unanswered. Here we apply the Scripture, ". . . taking every thought captive to the obedience of Christ" (2 Cor. 10:5). This section is one more way to capture thoughts that stream off in the wind like an April kite, reeling them in with soul-searching questions.

Hymns of Praise

Music is an integral part of the spirit, loosening our self-conscious soul-restraints and drawing us toward God. A poster in a choir room choruses, "He who sings, prays twice," and music is an appropriate prayer response to the infilling of Light. At each retreat, a hymnal is a wise companion. Take time to sing and worship through favorite hymns. Consider writing meaningful lyrics on 3×5 cards, worshiping with these on a walk. Other hymns may be committed to memory.

Praise music or recorded hymns are also good ways to start the heart singing, and instrumentals are especially good background for times of meditation.

One great hymn of faith reinforces the subject of the retreat, a reminder of the path we walked hand in hand with our Savior and Shepherd.

But . . . What About the Kids?!

Given the complex roles we as women play, finding time alone in any amount stretches our resources, one of which is our sanity. The challenges of raising children, running a home, maintaining a career, building a marriage: all compete for our attention. The ideal scenario is working together with a spouse to ensure each other a day or morning of soul-space each month. The ideal, however, quickly fades in the face of reality.

Reality may well be a disinterested or unavailable husband, or no husband at all. Raising children alone occupies every available ounce of energy—after providing food for the table. How can we possibly fit in more time, or in some cases, any time, for spiritual maintenance and growth?

Another question might be, how long can we ignore the gnawing emptiness in our hearts? *Quiet Places* is versatile. Twenty minutes over lunch; a brief respite before Junior awakens from his too-short, too-infrequent nap; or bartering with the children on Saturday morning for an hour's peace: all of these offer possibilities. (The benefits of one mother's year-long quiet times outside went beyond observing God's creative genius from the patio!) If paying for a baby-sitter is out of the question, consider trading children one morning every other week with another mom, or a Saturday switch twice a month. Check with women in your Bible study, parenting group, neighborhood, or Sunday school to work out more extended time alone.

A Word About Reentry

Moving into the world of the personal retreat can be difficult; moving out of that place of solitude back through the revolving doors of rush-hour living can foster immediate regression. It's easy to turn into horn-honking, red-faced drivers snarled in traffic.

The best safeguard against the crashing together of opposing worlds is to assume two things: the condition of our homes will be worse than our worst imaginings; and our children will be healthy but will still need a bath.

Keeping a vise-grip on the soul-benefits of the day, determine not to look at the deterioration. Focus instead on the lovely people waiting with open arms. They are watching for the positive aspects of being without their wife and/or mother; this is the time to demonstrate that the hours away from them reap blessings for the entire family.

CHAPTER ONE

Busyness and the False Self: Do and Do

Frantic activity is the facade worn to keep from meeting the woman behind the mask. Who are we without our incessant activities? This retreat invites us to find out.

Early morning silence muffled the rolling hills. Even the grain elevator dozed in these prelight moments. Hauling stiffly out of bed, I crept downstairs so as not to awaken a sleeping baby and preschooler. "Why didn't you get up earlier?" the internal Censor sneered. Already I dreaded the sound of little child feet. Hunger for space cloaked me with frustration like a terry-cloth robe.

A fluorescent glow sliced beneath Rich's office door. He must have awakened hours ago. Shrugging, I continued down the steps and into the kitchen.

While the coffee perked, I settled at the table with Bible and journal. In his first appointment as an ordained minister, Rich logged eighty-hour weeks pastoring two churches in this rural area. Much of the overflow

spilled onto these aching shoulders. Many church-related phone calls, er-
rands, and meetings crowded and confused my parenting and my personal
ministry interests. An unfinished list of things to do begged for attention.

Glancing at the list, a sigh escaped. I turned to the Scriptures. The
familiar yearning for God's voice, the longing to hear His whispers again,
spread through the country quiet.

The peace was short-lived. In minutes Rich whistled his way down the
stairs and into the gingham kitchen, the hub of our home. I looked up,
trying not to be unfriendly.

"Hon, could you help with a few things today?" Rich half asked, half
stated, his puppy-dog eyes convincing.

My own glance moved from the Bible to yesterday's list to the scribbled
paper offered. Like a shaken bottle of soda pop, the frustration within exploded. Too many days of pouring out for other people's needs, too little
time refilling took its inevitable toll. Like a spectator, I listened in horror
to the words foaming from my mouth.

"All I ever do is bail you out! Everything is an emergency. Well, forget
it. I don't have a life." Anger's adrenaline flooded my body, screaming for
an outlet. Grabbing the empty high chair, I slammed it into the cracked
linoleum, shouting after his now-retreating back, "What do you think I
am? Your servant?"

I regarded my hands as if they had a life of their own, as if they be-
longed to a stranger. Shaking, I released the crooked high chair and sank
into a seat. Tears rivered down hot cheeks. My head dropped on my fore-
arms. "Where's the calm, cool, collected minister's wife now?" the Censor
jeered.

The high-chair episode forced the beginnings of an ongoing healing
process. I had to choose between healing and self-destruction, between
family preservation and busyness, between sanity and soul-suicide. The
choice continues to be difficult, the process in turns painful and fruitful.

A third child joined us in the intervening years, and we are several
churches beyond that rural time. Recently, trying to make room in a
crowded file cabinet, I paused over old calendars. The squares and pages
were covered with ink, a scribbled chronology of deliberate insanity. Not
one blank space stared out from all the documented years.

My life is not much different than anyone else's. When I speak to wom-
en's groups, no one ever raises their hand to the question "Who in this
room is *not* busy?" We are a frantic people, running some nonstop mar-
athon that someone else organizes and signs us up for. Our sides hitch,
our breath comes in racking gasps, and our heart pounds. When we lie

down at night, we either collapse from exhaustion or roll an endless progression of duties, commitments, and to do's past our mind's eye.

Busyness is epidemic. The reasons behind our busyness vary, but rarely are they the ones most often cited. "My kids, their activities," one mother says, raising her shoulders helplessly. "Everyone needs me," another laments, pulling a flip phone out of her purse to call home. Checking the beeper vibrating at her waistband, a woman sighs, "Always on call."

For me, this frantic activity was a facade, worn to keep from meeting the real me, the woman hidden behind the mask. What if I didn't like the person cowering behind the false mask of busyness? Who would she be without all the activities? It was a question I didn't want to face.

Busyness lends a false sense of importance to our days. If we're busy, we rationalize, we must be valuable. Being needed—by husband, child, employer, friend, church—is far more comfortable than facing the gaunt emptiness of our own souls. This perpetual churning thinly covers the lack of meaning, shielding us from our fear of nothingness. It also substitutes for waiting on God. Afraid of saying no to the wrong thing, we feel compelled to say yes to everything.

The only antidote I have found to busyness is solitude. The purpose of retreat is not to check off a list of Scriptures read, quotes studied, or prayers said. It is an escape into the calm arms of God.

And because busyness sedates the underlying reality, when we hurtle through life's revolving doors into a personal retreat time, we may feel confused, uncomfortable, awkward via the lack of agenda, the aloneness, the "not doing."

The desert mothers and fathers forsook the busyness, the meaninglessness and materialism of the world, exchanging it for a world of solitude, contemplation, intercession. They shed the mask of self-importance and entered the desert. There they found an oasis of refreshment, food for soul and spirit.

Several years ago, the air vibrated with the drone of locusts, reminiscent of pre-Exodus plagues. On a walk around the neighborhood, one could see empty shells clinging to tree bark, hiding in green grasses, crunching underfoot on the sidewalk. Every June of my childhood I collected these translucent hollows. Now, as an adult, the locust has become a metaphor, leaving behind a shell that no longer fits, a lifestyle that outlived its usefulness.

The shell of busyness hasn't been shed in its entirety, left behind like discarded baggage. No, the crust still clings to my back, broken edges pinching and piercing, and I drag it along, comfortable in my discomfort.

But through the cracks and the chips, the exposed new skin breathes and expands; these spaces for soul-expansion feel good. I try to create large chunks of time for resting in God, even while searching for other, smaller spaces to shed particles of the shell of busyness; a few minutes in the morning, a paragraph read while waiting, a Scripture savored at a stoplight, deep breaths while I focus only on God's love for me.

May this personal retreat be a time when the shell of busyness begins to crack and chip, where soul-thirst is both quenched and renewed, where dehydrated spirits and arid lives are restored.

Quotes for Contemplation

Solitude is the furnace of transformation. Without solitude we remain victims of our society and continue to be entangled in the illusions of the false self. Jesus himself entered into this furnace. There he was tempted with the three compulsions of the world: to be relevant ("turn stones to bread"), to be spectacular ("throw yourself down"), and to be powerful ("I will give you all these kingdoms").

—HENRI NOUWEN,
THE WAY OF THE HEART

Call often to mind the proverb that "The eye is not satisfied with seeing, nor the ear filled with hearing." Endeavor therefore to withdraw thy heart from the love of visible things and to turn thyself to the invisible.

—THOMAS À KEMPIS,
THE IMITATION OF CHRIST

Busyness rapes relationships.
It substitutes shallow frenzy for deep friendships.
It promises satisfying dreams, but delivers hollow
    nightmares.
It feeds the ego, but starves the inner man.
It fills the calendar, but fractures the family.
It cultivates a program, but plows under priorities.

—ANONYMOUS

There is the ultimate danger inherent in our humanity always to assume that whatever it is we do, whatever it is that absorbs us . . . that these things are the center of the world. Our professions become primary. . . . Anything that preoccupies our attention can eventually slip into that cavity in our souls in an attempt to fill the spot that was meant only for One Other to indwell.

—**KAREN BURTON MAINS**,
KAREN KAREN

The struggle is real because the danger is real. It is the danger of living the whole of our life as one long defense against the reality of our condition, one restless effort to convince ourselves of our virtuousness. Yet Jesus "did not come to call the virtuous, but sinners" (Matt. 9:13).

—**HENRI NOUWEN**,
THE WAY OF THE HEART

We must have some room to breathe. We need freedom to think and permission to heal. Our relationships are being starved to death by velocity. No one has the time to listen, let alone love. Our children lie wounded on the ground, run over by our high-speed good intentions. Is God now pro-exhaustion? Doesn't He lead people beside the still waters anymore?

—**RICHARD A. SWENSON**,
MARGIN

The dissolution of both society and our personal lives is disguised behind the noise of the world.

—**JANE A. RUBIETTA**

The pace of life and our preoccupation with unimportant things take so much of our attention. The significant things, like taking time to develop friendships, to read [the Bible] and pray, to read books that are challenging, to listen to God—these all get sacrificed on the altar of good works and Christian busyness.

—**LUCI SHAW**,
QUOTED IN VIRTUE

I need wide spaces in my heart
Where Faith and I can go apart
And grow serene.
Life gets so choked by busy living,
Kindness so lost in fussy giving
That Love slips by unseen.

—**ANONYMOUS**

Scriptures for Meditation

"This is the resting place, let the weary rest";
and, "This is the place of repose"—
  but they would not listen.
So then, the word of the Lord to them will become:
  Do and do, do and do,
    rule on rule, rule on rule.

—ISAIAH 28:12–13, NIV

Find rest, O my soul, in God alone;
  my hope comes from him.
He alone is my rock and my salvation;
  he is my fortress, I will not be shaken.
My salvation and my honor depend on God;
  he is my mighty rock, my refuge.

—PSALM 62:5–7, NIV

You must deny yourselves and do no work.

—NUMBERS 29:7, NIV

Gracious is the Lord, and righteous;
Yes, our God is compassionate. . . .
Return to your rest, O my soul,
For the Lord has dealt bountifully with you.

—PSALM 116:5, 7

Thus says the Lord,
"Stand by the ways and see and ask for the ancient paths,
Where the good way is, and walk in it;
And you shall find rest for your souls."

—JEREMIAH 6:16

Journaling

Now would be a good time to journal. Some starter suggestions:
1. What primary thought about busyness nudges right now?
2. Think about the Scriptures; where did the Spirit seem to highlight specific areas?
3. What is your primary reaction? Write some of the reasons behind that

reaction. What is the Lord trying to say to you now?

4. Where did the quotes for contemplation stir you? Can you spend some time thinking with your pen about that?

Prayers of Confession, Praise, Petition

Prayer can be sprinkled throughout the process of personal retreat; this is ideal. Still, it's easy to let all the reading and writing squeeze out prayer time.

Take some time now to confess your sins to God, to praise Him, and to ask for God's loving action in others' lives.

Moments for Creation

Walking outside, enjoying creation, during or after the time of prayer, draws us closer to our Creator. Make some time now, or later, to walk, observe, pray. Take a "Praise and Thanksgiving Walk," or carry a hymn or two along to "make a joyful noise" as you experience God's presence outdoors. You may want to gather a keepsake—a leaf, stone, flower—to remind you of the path you walked with God.

Silence

"Cease striving and know that I am God; I will be exalted among the nations, I will be exalted in the earth" (Ps. 46:10). Spend time now in silence. You might begin with a phrase about God, such as "You are worthy" or "Christ have mercy," or a phrase from Scripture, such as, "The Lord is my shepherd."

When finished, jot down impressions you received during the silence, as well as how it felt, where you were frustrated, etc.

Questions for Reflection

1. When do you feel the crunch of busyness? How does it affect you? Why do you keep really busy?

2. How do you feel about setting up a personal retreat day? What would healthy soul-care look like for you, ideally?

3. Where do you find true rest? Perhaps you believe that your salvation comes from God, but do you live like it? Where does your hope come from? Children, husband, work, hobbies?

4. How do you feel about solitude? How important is it to you to make room for solitude?

Hymn of Praise

TAKE TIME TO BE HOLY

Take time to be holy, speak oft with thy Lord;
Abide in Him always, and feed on His Word;
Make friends of God's children, help those who are weak,
Forgetting in nothing His blessing to seek.

Take time to be holy, the world rushes on;
Spend much time in secret with Jesus alone;
By looking to Jesus, like Him thou shalt be;
Thy friends in thy conduct His likeness shall see.

Take time to be holy, let Him be thy guide,
And run not before Him, whatever betide;
In joy or in sorrow, still follow thy Lord,
And, looking to Jesus, still trust in His Word.

Take time to be holy, be calm in thy soul,
Each thought and each motive beneath His control;
Thus, led by His spirit to fountains of love
Thou soon shalt be fitted for service above.

—**WILLIAM D. LONGSTAFF**

CHAPTER TWO

Mending the Broken Mirror

Too many of us view our worth in God's eyes through a warped and distorted mirror, which determines the way we live. Here we look in the mirror and begin to mend the brokenness we see there.

As I browsed the fabric store, a sale table lured me toward the doorway. The myriad hues, textures, and colors soothed my overstretched brain and inspired my creativity. My mother tutored me in the fine art of sewing at a tender age, and because of a ridiculously long inseam, I would always need to make my own slacks. When the bells over the door jangled, I glanced up idly. The girl entered with her mother. Her legs seemed to come clear to my rib cage. They were long and ultrathin, almost wavy. She had to be seven and a half feet tall. With my own frame nearing the two-yard line, she towered over me, even bent over as she was like a spoon. Her mother supported her as they threaded their way through the bolts and notions.

Incredible sadness overwhelmed me. Politeness dictated a return to fabric inspection, but the thudding of my heart stole my attention. Glancing at the child one last time, at her mother who guided her in selecting suitable materials, I beat a path to the door and walked home. Once there, I wanted to throw myself on my bed and sob, to pound my fists and cry like a small child from a deep, deep wound.

I did neither, but depression trailed me like bad weather. Eventually, I scrolled through my day to locate the cause. The cursor in my brain kept locking up at the trip to the fabric store, and I knew I had to look deeper.

In my mind I saw the girl weaving through the store; then the image changed, and I saw myself in her body. A reel of childhood memories shone on the internal screen: cruel chants from faceless children, calling me Bird Legs. A picture from high school, looking like a recent release from Dachau. The grueling search for clothes that fit; the agony of being the latest of late bloomers, of crying on my mother's shoulder on prom night, "I really wanted to go," and the grace of her tactful, loving presence.

Nearly incapacitating shyness delayed my social skills; I saw a person with no opinions, no likes and dislikes, no mind of her own. Being in an elevator with two strangers was torment; what if they said hello? What would I say in return? How could I possibly initiate dialogue, even meaningless chitchat, with strangers? Or for that matter, with adults I knew? I would struggle with meaningful, in-depth conversation for a lifetime.

Looking in the mirror at age thirty-one, with a string of interesting accomplishments trailing me, I did not see a tall, reasonably attractive brunette with talents and capabilities, able to run a home, raise children, and work with a growing marriage; able to lead a Bible study and counsel other women and get down on a child's level and communicate meaningfully. I certainly didn't see someone made in the image of God.

The looking glass reflected, instead, an emotionally deformed woman. Clearly I needed a new mirror.

Self-Esteem: The Battle of the Broken Mirror

The woman sat across from me, ancient and wizened and with a hearing aid in one ear. She had dedicated her life to listening to the Lord, and we arranged to meet together. We discussed various spiritual concerns of mine, including an inability to follow through on priorities, especially that of prayer. Out of nowhere, or so it seemed, she asked, "Do you believe God really loves you? You?"

At the stunned expression on my face, she smiled and her eyes crinkled. "Of course God loves everyone, but how about just you? Do you believe that you are special in God's sight?"

"Intellectually, yes. But emotionally, not always." An embarrassing thing for a pastor's wife to admit, but I let the statement stand.

Deep down, I recognized that not only did I truly dislike myself but I believed that with or without Jesus Christ, God couldn't really like me, much less love me. This seems, to me, to be the crux of the battle of the broken mirror.

Self-esteem as a topic has been hammered mercilessly into the ground. But healthy self-esteem, or self-love, as some label it, is fundamental to our ability to know God's love. It is a prerequisite to experiencing and expressing forgiveness, to setting boundaries, even to allowing ourselves the space we need to grow spiritually and emotionally. In my own life, with the mirror I used to view myself, it was impossible to receive God's love and in turn give it out with this crippled understanding of my value in God's sight.

In an era when women accomplish super careers and raise super children and run around in super circles in churches and communities, one would think epidemic low self-esteem had been inoculated out of existence, much like smallpox. But as I talk with women, occasionally they lower their Wow-what-a-woman! facade to reveal their humanness. Behind the efficiency, the competence, and the high IQs are women, like me, with a twisted, wounded image of themselves. It's the *image* we dislike, not the reality. Like the eighty-five-pound anorexic who sees an overweight woman in her mirror, we see someone we can't love.

The New Idolatry

"But I'm not supposed to love myself. It's not spiritual," the woman wailed. "It sounds indulging and paganistic."

Her counselor nodded, eyes loving and wise. "Do you think instead you're supposed to hate yourself?"

A telling silence followed. Few people I know would espouse a self-hatred approach to their spirituality, but there's a low-level discomfort with the term self-love. Do we essentially operate out of the assumption that loving ourselves is sinful? Could the opposite, in fact, be true: the lack of care and acceptance of ourselves is sinful?

Is low self-esteem not, in fact, a refusal to accept our basic humanity, to own the fact that our arrows will come short of the bull's-eye shot after shot, every time we pull the bowstring? If so, if we really believe we should be perfect, aren't we sinning along the same lines as Eve, with juice dripping over our fingers, waiting to become like God? Moving this thought toward logical completion, then, isn't low self-esteem—the inability to love ourselves because we can't be perfect—actually a perverse form of idolatry?

Might poor self-image also be a sign of our longing for perfection, for Eden in the midst of rocks and weeds and the onerous process of hoeing out a living?

Low self-esteem bears evidence as well of the mirror broken between us and God, of an essential chasm unbridgeable by all our efforts. At the roots of the crisis is both a lack of God-knowledge and of self-knowledge. In spite of a working familiarity with Scripture, my experience of God was largely warped, a contorted image in a carnival mirror. I recognized that at the core of my being, parts of me had never intersected with the Lord of the universe.

By the very act of Creation, God determined and even stated our worth. King Solomon, at the dedication of the temple, asks, "Will God indeed dwell with mankind on the earth? Behold, heaven and the highest heaven cannot contain Thee; how much less this house which I have built" (2 Chron. 6:18). Not only did Jesus assume the constrictions and limitations of a body like ours, but He cleansed us internally so that this God, whom the highest heavens cannot contain, might dwell within us. Thus Paul speaks of our bodies as the temple of the Holy Spirit. Who are we to condemn ourselves as unlovable, when God himself chooses our souls for His dwelling place? What insolence, to refute the very home in which Christ abides.

Is self-hatred not the ultimate slap in the face of God?

The self-esteem crisis also has its roots in a lack of self-knowledge. Days could pass before I formulate an opinion on a current event; I can deliberate for hours trying to understand what I feel and what I think. But, as we become conversant with the God of the Bible, as we become literate in self-understanding, the mirror begins to mend and we see ourselves as God sees us.

A discipline I attempt each year is to read through the Bible. A steady reading plan, like a one-year Bible, helps me stay on track. When I miss a day, I know I'll pick it up the next time through. One of the most healing exercises I've found for a clouded, distorted self-image is to underline in a special color of ink each passage that speaks of God's love for me. This year-long journey has brought me more deeply into a loving relationship with my heavenly Father. When the mirror becomes God's Word, the image in that mirror begins to change.

Do Less, Be More

The search for significance has directed our feet down paths of greater accomplishments, which is not necessarily bad. Unfortunately, to feel better about ourselves we place increasing pressure on our performance. Whether we perform in the home or in hallowed courtrooms or the school kitchen, if our mirrors reflect society's values rather than God's and our own, our search for significance continues to be blurred and barren. Meanwhile, the returns on our expanding investments of time and energy ever diminish.

Our relationships are a quest to find the kind of acceptance not based on performance. Deep within, a pearl of longing forms from the grains of life's irritations: accept me for who I am. Give me permission to fail, to grow, to learn, to love, to start over, to heal. Take away the need to do more in order to feel better about myself. At a ladies' retreat, a woman summed it up simply: to do less, and to be more.

We cannot afford to equate success with performance. Jesus Christ abolished forever the need to perform when He purchased all of our failures, at the cost of His own life, on the cross.

Deny Yourselves

During college, the deaths of seven people I knew, some of whom I loved dearly, brought me to a new and meaningful encounter with Christ. I set about to follow Him steadily. For a few months I landed in the middle of a rigid, no-gray-areas type of church, which suited my black-and-white approach to life just fine. Comfortable with thou-shalt-nots, I encountered a God and a people who seemed to thrive on rules. One of my favorite bits of Bible-out-of-context were Jesus' words, "If anyone wishes to come after Me, let him deny himself, and take up his cross, and follow Me" (Mark 8:34).

This section crouches in the middle of a chapter on broken mirrors of the soul for a good reason. At the heart of this is a dilemma. Deep down, we may well believe that self-love is the very opposite of what Jesus taught about self-denial. How then do we deal with the two most important commandments in the world? For Jesus also said, " 'You shall love the Lord your God with all your heart, and with all your soul, and with all your mind.' This is the great and foremost commandment. The second is like it, 'You shall love your neighbor as yourself' " (Matt. 22:37–39).

If our love for our neighbor is determined by our love for ourselves, many of us are engaged in battles to rival any gang warfare across the country. The truth is sobering: to love others and not love ourselves is hypocrisy; to love God and not love ourselves is blasphemy.

Denying oneself cannot be one and the same with self-hatred. Rather, self-love must be the plumb line, the measuring rod, that determines how well we love others.

Some confusion exists about what self-denial actually is. Leann, a writer, says, "Our former church taught this about self-denial: If you are good at something, then God would not call you to minister in that area because then you'd be going on your own strength and not God's." Another, a teacher in a Christian school, laments, "This church believes that self-denial is driving out pride. No one would ever say, 'That's a great bulletin board! Good job,' because the teacher might feel pride. Consequently, there's absolutely no affirmation for using God-given creativity."

Is self-denial denying or ignoring the innate gifts and talents provided by our Creator? Is it refusing to recognize our need for God's love and affirmation? Or is it, perhaps, refusing to wallow in the self-imposed abyss of self-hatred and neglect? Might it be refusing to indulge ourselves in over-emoting? Could self-denial mean denying ourselves the opportunity to fritter away our lives on meaningless activities, focusing instead on the most important aspects of our earthly lives: loving our God, and loving our neighbor as ourselves?

As we think about self-denial, shame raises its serpent head.

Shame and the Self

"We had a five-year honeymoon," says Marcie of her marriage to Robert. "We were so happy. But Robert said over and over, 'I don't deserve to be this happy.' "

Inside many of us is a shame-based voice that continually says, "I don't deserve this" or "I'm not worth taking the time (or money, or effort) to . . ." (Fill in the blank: receive counsel, go out for lunch, take a class, go on a personal retreat, hire a sitter to attend a recovery group, etc.)

This voice of shame alternately howls, "You're so stupid!" or "You can't possibly do that!" or whispers an insidious, "What a mess you are!" Shame's other favorite phrases are "Oh, you don't have to pay me" or "Please take advantage of me" or "My time isn't worth anything" or "You don't do this—or anything—well." Whatever the words, shame's underlying message is always the same: you don't deserve to be loved.

Shame undermines one's sense of value in God's sight, or one's talents and capabilities. Shame ruins the mercury behind the glass that makes up our mirrors.

It's time to reback our soul-mirrors, to align our self-images with a more accurate vision of how our Creator sees and loves us.

Like any good thing, however, self-esteem can be taken to an unhealthy extreme.

Self-Esteem vs. Self-Absorption

According to Greek mythology, Narcissus, the son of the handsome River God, was distinguished by his beauty. A seer told his mother that Narcissus would live a long life if he never gazed at his own features. One day, Narcissus wandered to the water's edge. Seeing his appealing countenance for the first time, he fell in love with his image and pined away, trapped by his love for his own reflection.

Modern-day narcissism, rooted in the story of Narcissus, is defined as a morbid condition in which the subject is intensely interested in his own body. Our current society has been termed narcissistic because of the tendency to focus on ourselves and our own needs to the exclusion of our neighbors and of our God.

The fragile bloom of the narcissus reminds us of the danger of being trapped in our image, of gazing at ourselves too intently. Introspection is healthy; learning who we are, what we like, where we hurt, is vital to self-understanding and the healing of our warped self-images. But like some paranoid queen constantly demanding, "Who's the fairest one of all?" comparing ourselves with others, focusing on our own deficits, we miss God's loving presence within us and within others. There is a time for introspection, but the healthy individual balances this inward look by moving beyond herself, shifting her gaze to others.

The temptation will be to focus on others to the exclusion of ourselves.

Mirrors of Our Inner Selves

Centuries ago, King Solomon wrote, "As he thinks within himself, so he is" (Prov. 23:7). When a woman mutters, "Stupid, stupid, stupid"—about herself or her actions—the mirror reflects not a new creation but a soul distorted by poor self-image. In the first century Publilius Syrus said, "Speech is a mirror of the soul; as a man speaks, so is he." Hearing a woman use coarse language, I wonder about her feelings of self-esteem, that she would lower herself to speak in such a self-denigrating fashion.

In my own life, I found at least two mirrors that indicated an inability to believe that God loved me deeply as His child. The first was my unwillingness to accept compliments.

In response to someone's words, "You did a good job" or "That color looks good on you" or "You're a good parent," I inevitably denied their affirmation. Finally, I realized that refusing to receive a compliment seemed to be a rebuff of the one voicing an opinion, an aspersion on their taste or good sense or discernment.

After that, I decided to try an ultraholy reply, such as, "No, no, give thanks to God." Perhaps I thought a simple "Thank you" would make me vain. A mentor quickly set me straight. "Do you mean you can take no credit? Did you listen to God? Did you not prepare for forty hours? Were you faithful to employ the gifts you've been given? Then thank them, *and* thank God."

A second mirror displaying a poor understanding of God's love was my own poor self-care. With an allergy to certain staples, flour being one of them, a typical sandwich lunch for the children left me with no meal. Too often I prepared a lovely flour-laden main course, and then sat down at the table with no food to eat. Surely this self-neglect represents self-contempt, not healthy self-love. Neither does it represent true self-denial.

This, I regret to say, is not an area of total healing for me. Too often, thinking of myself as an afterthought means that I go without something fundamental for my well-being, whether the area is emotional, physiological, or spiritual.

Learning to identify areas that blur our sense of value in God's eyes is a vital step toward a new image in the mirror.

A New Mirror

Not long after seeing myself in the girl with the chromosomal abnormality in the fabric store, I attended my regular self-help group. Throughout the meeting, I felt Stuart's gaze on me, not in a leering manner but almost as an artist studies a still life before beginning to paint.

After the meeting, I slipped away and hurried through the crowd, shy, and reticent to initiate conversation. Stuart stopped me several feet from the door.

"Jane. Just a minute. I wanted to ask you, have you ever been a model?"

Acute embarrassment colored my cheeks and twisted my tongue. "Well, no. I, uh, did some runway work, very small-time stuff, in college, but no—" I broke off, not knowing where this would lead.

"I'm a professional photographer, and I just kept looking at you and felt you must be very photogenic. Eyes, cheekbones . . ."

Immediately I began to ward off his assessment. "I don't know about photogenic—"

"Well, I do. I feel I'm qualified to talk about it." He shared some of his publishing triumphs. Then, seeing my discomfort, Stuart backed away. "That's all I wanted to say."

In the car, I thought back to that little girl who felt ugly, deformed, abnormal, and I heard the Lord gently telling me, "You are precious, Jane. Don't look at the old image anymore. Look in my mirror."

During this time, I invite you to look into your own inner mirrors, to inspect the image you display, and then to look to God's mirror.

Quotes for Contemplation ―――――――――――――――――――

Confidence is knowing and accepting ourselves so we can forget ourselves.

—JOANNE WALLACE[1]

Self-esteem is the human hunger for the divine dignity that God intended to be our emotional birthright as children created in his image.

—ROBERT SCHULLER,
SELF-ESTEEM: THE NEW
REFORMATION

How inconceivable it is to really love others (not merely to need them), if one cannot love oneself as one really is. And how could a person do that if, from the very beginning, he has had no chance to express his true feelings and to learn to know himself?

—ALICE MILLER,
PRISONERS OF CHILDHOOD: THE
DRAMA OF THE GIFTED CHILD AND
THE SEARCH FOR THE TRUE SELF

Our courteous Lord does not want his servants to despair, even when they sin: for our falling does not hinder his loving.

—JULIAN OF NORWICH

When He talks of losing their selves, He means only abandoning the clamor of self-will; once they have done that, He really gives them back all their personality, and boasts (I am afraid, sincerely) that when they are wholly His they will be more themselves than ever.

—C. S. LEWIS,
THE SCREWTAPE LETTERS

Drivenness is an insatiable drive to do more. . . . It's a drive that may be masked by charitable and positive motives, but in reality originates in deep, perhaps even unconscious, feelings of inadequacy and shame.

—DRS. ROBERT HEMFELT, FRANK
MINIRTH, AND PAUL MEIER,
WE ARE DRIVEN: THE COMPULSIVE
BEHAVIOR AMERICA APPLAUDS

Scriptures for Meditation

This is how much God loved the world: He gave his Son, his one and only Son. And this is why: so that no one need be destroyed; by believing in him, anyone can have a whole and lasting life. God didn't go to all the trouble of sending his Son merely to point an accusing finger, telling the world how bad it was. He came to help, to put the world right again. Anyone who trusts in him is acquitted; anyone who refuses to trust him has long since been under the death sentence without knowing it.

—JOHN 3:16–18,
THE MESSAGE

Thou didst form my inward parts;
Thou didst weave me in my mother's womb.
I will give thanks to Thee, for I am fearfully
*   and wonderfully made;*
Wonderful are Thy works,
And my soul knows it very well.

—PSALM 139:13–14

Therefore if anyone is in Christ, he is a new creature; the old things passed away; behold, new things have come.

—2 CORINTHIANS 5:17

"Can a woman forget her nursing child,
And have no compassion on the son of her womb?
Even these may forget, but I will not forget you.
Behold, I have inscribed you on the palms of My hands."

—ISAIAH 49:15–16

*It's in Christ that we find out who we are and what we are living for.
Long before we first heard of Christ and got our hopes up, he had his eye
on us, had designs on us for glorious living, part of the overall purpose he
is working out in everything and everyone.*

— EPHESIANS 1:11–12,
THE MESSAGE

*How great is the love the Father has lavished on us, that we should be
called children of God! And that is what we are!*

—1 JOHN 3:1, NIV

*"I have loved you with an everlasting love;
I have drawn you with loving-kindness."*

—JEREMIAH 31:3, NIV

Journaling

Use this as a time to plumb the depths to see how you really feel about
your standing in Christ. Has there been a time in your life when you really
exchanged your life for Christ's, when you accepted His sacrificial death
on the cross in your place?

Where do you see evidence of being a new creation (2 Cor. 5:17)?

Are there old images of yourself that need to be renewed?

Prayers of Confession, Praise, Petition

Consider the FACT that God loves you enough to die for you. Imagine!
God on a cross. As you evaluate your beliefs about your value in the Lord's
sight, compare those beliefs with what the Lord says in His Word. This
should lead you into a time of relief and heartfelt praise! From there, ask
the Holy Spirit to make a clean sweep of your soul, bringing residual sin
to mind. Confess those sins, and praise Him for the gracious forgiveness
granted. Petition is simply bringing your requests before the throne of
grace. May you receive grace and mercy during this time of prayer.

Moments for Creation

Do you feel sluggish? Take time to nap, to truly rest in the grace of
God. If a gentle walk is the answer, head for the outdoors. Once there,
observe the wildlife you see around you. What animals or birds seem to

have a crisis of self-worth? Note the order in creation; invite the Holy Spirit to open your eyes as you walk. You might want to take some 3×5 cards with you to jot down thoughts you had during your time outside.

Silence

Think of the Scriptures on which you contemplated earlier. Which one sticks in your mind, eagerly reminding you of God's great esteem for you in Christ Jesus? Move into a time of silence as you consider that overwhelming, totally accepting love.

Questions for Reflection

1. Take time to look into the mirror of your soul. What do you see? How do you really feel about yourself? Be honest. This is between you and God alone.

2. What has been revealed to you in Scripture about yourself? About God?

3. Are there Scriptures that remind you how great the love is that God has lavished on you? Where has God's love been revealed?

4. Think back to the person you saw in the mirror. What are evidences of low self-esteem as you study your life and choices? For instance, do you saddle yourself with poor, degrading, self-defeating relationships, or surround yourself with people who bleed you dry? Do you refuse to take time to grow in areas of personal interest?

5. For an exercise in self-esteem, list some *needs* you have. (For example, I NEED a good friend, I NEED to eat better, I NEED to see a dentist, I NEED time with a counselor or spiritual mentor. . . .)
   Taking care of our needs is healthy. In addition, it validates God's

love and interest in us. What is God nudging you to do?

Hymn of Praise ———————————————————

AND CAN IT BE THAT I SHOULD GAIN?

And can it be that I should gain
An interest in the Savior's blood!
Died He for Me? who caused His pain!
For me? who Him to death pursued?
Amazing love! How can it be
That Thou, my God, shouldst die for me?
Amazing love! How can it be
That Thou, my God, shouldst die for me?

'Tis mystery all: th'Immortal dies!
Who can explore His strange design?
In vain the firstborn seraph tries
To sound the depths of love divine.
'Tis mercy all! Let earth adore;
Let angel minds inquire no more.
'Tis mercy all! Let earth adore;
Let angel minds inquire no more.

He left His Father's throne above,
So free, so infinite his grace!
Emptied himself of all but love,
And bled for Adam's helpless race.
'Tis mercy all, immense and free,
For, O my God, it found out me!
'Tis mercy all, immense and free,
For, O my God, it found out me!

Long my imprisoned spirit lay,
Fast bound in sin and nature's night;
Thine eye diffused a quickening ray;
I woke, the dungeon flamed with light;
My chains fell off, my heart was free,
I rose, went forth, and followed thee.

My chains fell off, my heart was free,
I rose, went forth, and followed thee.

No condemnation now I dread;
Jesus, and all in Him, is mine;
Alive in Him, my living Head,
And clothed in righteousness divine.
Bold I approach th'eternal throne,
And claim the crown, through Christ my own.
Bold I approach th'eternal throne,
And claim the crown, through Christ my own.

—CHARLES WESLEY

Alternate Hymn

AMAZING GRACE

Amazing grace! How sweet the sound
That saved a wretch like me!
I once was lost, but now am found;
Was blind, but now I see.

'Twas grace that taught my heart to fear,
And grace my fears relieved;
How precious did that grace appear
The hour I first believed.

Through many dangers, toils, and snares,
I have already come;
'Tis grace hath brought me safe thus far,
And grace will lead me home.

The Lord has promised good to me,
His word my hope secures;
He will my shield and portion be,
As long as life endures.

When we've been there ten thousand years,
Bright shining as the sun;
We've no less days
To sing God's praise
Than when we first begun.

—JOHN NEWTON

CHAPTER THREE

A New Line Dance

Boundaries protect the special identity God has given us. When the boundaries are blurred, we no longer act out of the deepest sense of our being. In this retreat, we will consider how and where to "draw the line."

"Out of bounds!" the child cried. The ball bounced aimlessly through the ranks of eager playmates and rolled toward the far fence, out of play. Prior to the game, the kids paced off lines between trees and fences and stones, declaring anything beyond those lines "out of bounds."

Somehow, emerging from the spontaneous, adamant years of childhood, we lose that ability to cry, "Out of bounds!" We forget to run the bases. We're afraid to yell, "Foul ball!" in declaring someone else's behavior out of bounds. We fail to limit others' access to, and demands upon, us. We neglect to fix a border, to draw a separating line that defines where our territory ends and another's begins. "Nothing is impossible with God," we read, and gird up our loins. Surely it follows that nothing is impossible with us, either. "Victory in Jesus!" we shout, and on we run. Without boundaries, we gasp in an endless race.

According to Webster's, a boundary is something that indicates or fixes a limit or extent; specifically, a bounding or separating line. Drs. Robert Hemfelt and Paul Warren, in their book *Kids Who Carry Our Pain*, further define a boundary as "the invisible line that protects the special identity

God has given every child." But because the line is invisible, it is far too easy to allow trespassing.

My husband and I are considering the installation of an invisible fence. A transmitter is buried in our dog's fur and a wire in the ground, establishing boundaries for Shaka. Should she step over that invisible fence, she would immediately be shocked back into our yard, back into the safe boundaries determined for her. Outside the fencing, she poses a risk to herself because she isn't street-smart, and a risk to others because of her size. Across the shock line, she could be stolen or struck by a car or could wander beyond her ability to get back home. The dogcatcher, or a territorial homeowner with a BB gun, present further risks. Shaka needs a fence to protect her.

So do we.

In their book *Boundary Power*, Mike O'Neil and Charles Newbold sum up boundaries in one phrase: "I am not you." They go on to write, "My boundaries tell me who I am. Without a clear sense of boundaries, I am not going to know who I am. Boundaries and a sense of self go hand in hand. They are like maps that help us find our way down the road of life. They show us where the unsafe places are in relationships so we can avoid them, and they show us how to protect ourselves in all other areas of our lives."[1]

Many times in my life I have been unable to distinguish between my own thoughts, needs, and opinions and those of another; unable to discern my own motives for acting; unable to detect an underground fence over which I should not step. This occasional lapse in boundaries leaves me overwhelmed, angry, guilty, and depressed.

Unfortunately, the shock of stepping out of bounds is delayed for us humans. In the long run, crossing the invisible line weakens our self-identity and blurs our vision.

This lack of boundaries contributes not only to busyness and stress; the ramifications affect vital areas of our lives. Dr. John Townsend writes in *Hiding From Love*, "The problem of unclear boundaries is probably the [second] most serious cause of emotional and spiritual struggles experienced by Christians today. Depression, anxiety, feelings of powerlessness and helplessness, a diffused sense of identity and direction, and codependency problems are all linked to boundary deficits."[2]

When who we are becomes confused with what we do and what others think or expect of us, our boundary-line dance gets confused. We begin to do for others what they can do for themselves, taking responsibility for their needs rather than our own.

As Christians, we must learn the difference between being responsive to legitimate needs of others in our relationships and rescuing them from the consequences of their own behavior. Failure to do so damages both parties.

The spiritual ramifications of a lack of boundaries hurt us as well. A saying in the Twelve-Step tradition is that religion is the first to leave and the last to return. After establishing a boundary between ourselves and others, we can begin to find that oneness, that intimacy with God that so often eludes those without boundaries. When I learn to distinguish my own boundaries, then I begin to be an individual, capable of relating to an individual God.

Boundaries encompass all areas of our lives: emotional, spiritual, intellectual, physical, and sexual; family, work, and friends are all affected by boundaries. Boundary violations, write Drs. Henry Cloud and John Townsend, occur "when one trespasses on the other's personhood, when one crosses a line and tries to control the feelings, attitudes, behaviors, choices, and values of the other."[3]

Consider Leah, for example. She stood at the stove, supper simmering. The phone rang. Leah glanced at the clock and sighed, even as she reached for the receiver. She scrunched her shoulder to prop the phone and free her hands. Her mother's voice on the other end was no surprise. She always called at this time. Now supper would be late, the kids wouldn't be bathed, and the work she brought home would be pushed far into the night, eliminating needed time with her husband. The gnawing began in the pit of her stomach even as she answered. "Hi, Mom. No, no, this is a good time. I'm just fixing dinner."

Or Jan. Jan taught school for forty years, all the while collecting travel brochures and dreaming about retirement. Finally, she would be free to explore the world she'd only read and taught about. But after retiring, her son dumped her only grandchild into her lap, and she felt duty bound to care for the baby.

Or consider Anita. Anita was so busy proving to her husband and family that she could go on after a miscarriage, doing everything she'd previously done, that she nearly collapsed spiritually, physically, and emotionally.

Ramona was a hard worker with a tender heart. Demands at work outmuscled her commitment to her family, so when her job grew to encompass the work of two people, she simply did the work of two people. Sometimes, after working around the clock, she left the office to change her clothes just minutes before her co-workers returned from a good night's rest. She wasn't compensated for the extra time—her boss had no idea how many hours she worked—and she and her family paid many times over for the hours of work she plowed through at her dining-room table.

Leah, Jan, Anita, and Ramona are pseudonyms for you, for me, for women in general. Yes, they are real examples, and every town and city harbors them.

Limited access makes times of accessibility all the more precious; by creating boundaries, we create, in a sense, value. Our boundaries declare: we are worthy, our skills and gifts and needs are important and God-given, and sharing them with others is valuable. A primary problem with boundaries is that they are invisible; unless we alert passersby that they are in effect, those boundaries will be ignored.

No Faster, Please

In Germany, the signs on the highways read, "Nicht schneller, bitte." No faster, please. A courteous request. Interestingly enough, the pileups on German autobahns can stretch for 100 cars. Since it's not a speed *limit*, drivers eat up the road, and their cars eat up the drivers.

But we are finite human beings, with built-in speed limits. We cannot live in defiance of our created finitude for long.

For all the signs posted, we still don't like limits—or boundaries. When the directions read, "Two pain-relief capsules every four hours," we figure three will eradicate the pain so we needn't break stride. If the doctor orders complete bed rest, we fudge a bit and do the laundry. When Clarisse came home from the hospital after major back surgery, the surgeon said, "You must have live-in care and may only walk using a walker." The next day, a neighbor found Clarisse lurching around the house alone, walker stowed in a corner.

Boundaries were God's idea. God limited the sea by creating land; He limited the night by creating day. Because trees would exhaust themselves blooming continually, He made boundaries on the fruit-bearing seasons, requiring a necessary period of shedding and dormancy. He created a boundary around each of us, called skin, that protects and contains all that we are.

Jesus, too, demonstrated boundaries in his life. He ate, slept, prayed, taught, confronted. He wasn't afraid of people's anger, and He clearly defined who He was. He erected boundaries that all the powers of hell could not cross.

The Better Part and Its Cost

Setting boundaries requires taking responsibility for everything within our own skin, for eliminating the litany of excuses for inadequate soul- and body-care. The story of Mary and Martha (Luke 10) represents choices that determined their attitudes, outlooks, and activities. Martha chose to stew in the kitchen, churning inside and out, angry to be saddled with the work while her sister huddled at Jesus' feet.

Mary, on the other hand, though aware of the necessity of food, implemented a policy I call "planned neglect": evaluating her primary purpose in life and streamlining her actions accordingly. The necessity of eating could be handled in due time without infringing on limited time with her Savior. She let go of the need to impress her guests with a massive feast, and so chose the "better part, which will not be taken away from her" (v. 42, NRSV).

Still, even with the best of intentions, as we begin to establish boundaries and choose the better part, failure is possible, even probable, particularly with deeply ingrained missteps in our life dance. Setting boundaries requires learning new steps in the dance of life, the dance of relationships; our own atrophied muscles may get sore, and in the process we may step on toes. Loved ones and bosses and acquaintances may not like the new steps, and it's hard to stand firm when others are angry or upset.

Guilt, a natural companion to change, attaches itself like an octopus around the legs, continually threatening to trip the line dancers. And "risk" always hauls along its competitor, "worry," to cut in on the dance. "Maybe they won't like me when I change," we think. "Maybe I'll lose my job or my friends or . . ."

Perhaps we will. But maybe, just maybe, we'll create a new dance that eventually feels fair and healthy and spiritual.

Back to the Bases

Why do children run the bases in the beginning phases of their games? Do they run to fix the images and locations of the bases in their minds? To reinforce where the ball should go, and where it shouldn't? To acquire a taste for racing around the plates, beating the ball to each stop, heading for home and a home run?

Perhaps, today, we can run the bases in our minds, mentally outlining the boundaries of our lives, reinforcing what we will and will not do in relationship with others.

For, after all, how can we play ball if we don't know what's "out of bounds"?

Quotes for Contemplation ─────────────────────

The need to establish boundaries that allow us to say no is a mathematical necessity. With far too many demands and expectations upon us, we could not possibly fulfill them all, even should we desire to do so. Yet it is not easy to say no. With some, every time the word exits their mouths they have a crisis of guilt. The alternative, however, is acquiescing to the demand. Then, instead of a crisis of guilt, we have a crisis of margin depletion.

It is important to understand that most people simply are not sensitive. There is absence of malice but presence of callous. Other people's pain is invisible to them. Therefore, when they make demands upon us, they know not what they do.

We, then, must respond with grace, with sensitivity, yet with firmness: "I'm sorry, but I can't." To be able to say no without guilt is to be freed from one of the biggest monsters in our overburdened lives. If we decline, not out of self-serving laziness but for God-honoring balance and health, then this level of control will not only protect our emotional margin but will actually increase it.

—**RICHARD A. SWENSON,**
MARGIN

Boundary deficits can be deeply disabling to anyone, including Christians. People with unclear boundaries can find themselves making commitments under pressure that they would never make with a clear head. They find themselves "caving in" to others. They have trouble speaking their mind. They are afraid to be honest and tell the truth. They often can't protect themselves in injurious situations, such as being wrongly criticized. They are unable to stand firm and separate with their values, as Joshua did when he declared, "As for me and my house, we will serve the Lord" (24:15).

Unclear boundaries can also lead to a lack of direction in life. Boundaries are the conveyors of our personal power. People whose boundaries are underdeveloped find themselves floating along in their careers or relationships with no sense of initiative or goals.

The psychological fruits of these boundary problems can be devastating. Depression, anxiety, substance abuse, eating disorders, panic

*attacks, and identity disorders are a few of the results of boundary
conflicts.*

**—Dr. John Townsend,
Hiding From Love**

*How often we talk about boundaries. Most often these are boundaries
between us and other people. Where does my responsibility end and yours
start? But there are other boundaries—mental boundaries. One of them is
getting lost in yesterday.*

*Yesterday's fears can overrun the boundary of today like cattle through
a broken fence. We can lose sight of the difference between what
happened yesterday and what can happen today. We can allow yesterday's
resentments to become today's facts or yesterday's expectations to become
today's prophecies. Yesterday's people may become the people we deal with
today. Our fathers become our husbands or male friends. Patterns between
our mothers and their family systems become the expected norm for today.
It is unfair to do this to those around us now.*

*Today is a bright, new coin. It is potential, waiting for us to decide
what we shall spend it on. We have a choice, as always: yesterday's hurt or
today's celebration.*

**—Earnie Larsen and Carol
Larsen Hegarty,
Days of Healing, Days of Joy:
Daily Meditations
for Adult Children**

*We need to find maturing, caring people who will love our boundaries
just as much as they love our attachment. . . . Ask yourself, "Do the people
closest to me love my no as much as they love my yes?" If your no isn't
loved, then you aren't, either.*

**—Dr. John Townsend,
Hiding From Love**

*Who is stopping you from huddling at Jesus' feet? Why do you give
them the power to do so?*

—Jane A. Rubietta

*Healthy boundaries have some flexibility and some limits depending
upon the nature of the relationship. The roles we play in relationships
define the limits of appropriate interaction with others. Husbands and
wives have a different peer relationship with each other than the husband*

has with his golf partner. Co-workers have rules that apply on the job that are exclusive to the situation. Males relate to other males differently than females do to other female peers.

Our role with another person can change depending on the circumstances. We may be someone's boss on the job but a peer to him on a committee in our religious group. The role we play in relationships with others defines the boundaries that we set or accept.

We not only need to have healthy boundaries, but we also need to communicate to others what these boundaries are whether they know anything about boundaries or not. We don't have to buy Ronnie a teaching-tape series on boundaries for him to learn how to respect our boundaries. All we need to do is set our own boundaries and go on. We don't have to fix Ronnie. He can be mad, glad, or sad, and we can let him be that way. He can get over it or not get over it. Our boundary issues are about us, not about the other persons in our lives.

—**MIKE S. O'NEIL AND CHARLES E. NEWBOLD, BOUNDARY POWER: HOW I TREAT YOU, HOW I LET YOU TREAT ME, HOW I TREAT MYSELF**

Scriptures for Meditation

My beloved spoke, and said to me:
"Rise up, my love, my fair one,
And come away.
For, lo, the winter is past,
The rain is over and gone.
The flowers appear on the earth;
The time of singing has come,
And the voice of the turtledove
Is heard in our land.
The fig tree puts forth her green figs,
And the vines with the tender grapes
Give a good smell.
Rise up, my love, my fair one,
And come away!"

—**SONG OF SOLOMON 2:10–13, NKJV**

[Jesus] said to them, "Come with me by yourselves to a quiet place and get some rest."

—**Mark 6:31**, niv

"Who enclosed the sea with doors,
When, bursting forth, it went out from the womb;
When I made a cloud its garment,
And thick darkness its swaddling band,
And I placed boundaries on it,
And I set a bolt and doors,
And I said, 'Thus far you shall come, but no farther;
And here shall your proud waves stop'?"

—**Job 38:8–11**

He established the earth upon its foundations,
So that it will not totter forever and ever.
Thou didst cover it with the deep as with a garment;
The waters were standing above the mountains.
At Thy rebuke they fled;
At the sound of Thy thunder they hurried.
The mountains rose; the valleys sank down
To the place which Thou didst establish for them.
Thou didst set a boundary that they may not pass over;
That they may not return to cover the earth."

—**Psalm 104:5–9**

The lines have fallen to me in pleasant places;
Indeed, my heritage is beautiful to me.

—**Psalm 16:6**

Boundaries were created by God for our protection:

"And you shall set bounds for the people all around, saying, 'Beware that you do not go up on the mountain or touch the border of it; whoever touches the mountain shall surely be put to death.' "

—**Exodus 19:12**

Boundaries drive out enemies:

"And I will fix your boundary from the Red Sea to the sea of the

Philistines, and from the wilderness to the River Euphrates; for I will
deliver the inhabitants of the land into your hand, and you will drive
them out before you."

—EXODUS 23:31

Boundaries make us seek God:

"The God who made the world and all things in it . . . made from one,
every nation of mankind to live on all the face of the earth, having
determined their appointed times, and the boundaries of their habitation,
that they should seek God, if perhaps they might grope for Him and find
Him, though He is not far from each one of us; for in Him we live and
move and exist."

—ACTS 17:24, 26–28

God IS our boundary:

"In Him we live and move and exist."

—ACTS 17:28

Journaling

Sometime today create a place to think with the pen. What may the
Lord be telling you about boundaries? For instance, where did you feel the
prod of the Spirit while reading the opening reflection? At what point did
God quicken your heart while reading Scripture? Was there a time when
you felt tears begin, or anger, or joy? This is a safe place to put it in writing,
thus preserving a record of the Lord's work in your life, and your own work.

Prayers of Confession, Praise, Petition

Whether in your journal, out loud, or in your heart, begin the work of
heart-cleansing with a time of confession. Ask the Lord to bring to mind
places where sin might be crowding in a corner. Words of anger, spoken
in haste? Impatience, misplaced priorities, or focusing on an injustice?

Once the air is cleared with confession, dwell on the Lord, on His
bountiful forgiveness. Consider meditating on the subject of today's reflection. End with a time of petition.

Moments for Creation

Take some time to clear the cobwebs, warm the blood with a brisk walk
or a jog. Then slow down, contemplating the boundaries evidenced in

God's creation. You might want to bring the words to favorite hymns, or the lyrics to the hymn at the end of this chapter, to help you focus on what God has done on your behalf.

Silence

At some point, whether for fifteen seconds or fifteen minutes, spend some time in silence. You might want to read a psalm to concentrate your heart and mind on the Lord. Try Psalm 16 or 116. Read it several times slowly, then enter into silence before God.

Afterward, note in your journal what the Holy Spirit brought to mind. Don't be discouraged if thoughts intruded into the silence. Contemplative prayer takes practice.

Questions for Reflection

1. As you walk today, examine the created order for examples of boundaries God established. Look for the rationale behind the creative act. Where have you drawn boundaries in your own life? Consider emotional, spiritual, mental, and physical boundaries, as well as those related to work and family.

2. For follow-up, where *should* you draw boundary lines? For instance, can you draw a defining line around fifteen minutes of each day to spend before the Lord?

3. Who are the people in your life who continually trespass your boundary lines? What feelings wash over you when you permit trespassing? Consider two or three feeling statements you can make when someone vandalizes your interior property. (For example, "I feel angry when you don't listen to me" or "I feel unimportant when I tell you my work hours and you disregard them.")

4. Is there anyone in your life who deserves unlimited access to you?

Who, and why do you believe that is so? How does that fit in with what you know about boundaries?

5. What patterns from your parents do you see played out in your current relationships? Where did boundaries need to be established by your parents, and where have you followed in their uncomfortable dance shoes?

6. In seeking to determine boundaries, weigh your long-term goal as a Christian with all the short-term busyness of life. What will you plan to neglect? Perhaps lowering a housekeeping standard or an expectation about work. Where can you streamline? What choices about the running of a home, parenting, marriage, can you make to give your boundaries room?

7. Some people, whose boundaries have been repeatedly trampled, find it difficult to respect others' boundaries. Take some time to examine your close relationships: husband, children, friends, colleagues. Are there places where you trespass? How can you begin to respect others' boundaries as well?

Hymn of Praise

TAKE MY LIFE, AND LET IT BE

Take my life, and let it be consecrated, Lord, to Thee.
Take my moments and my days;
let them flow in ceaseless praise.
Take my hands, and let them move
at the impulse of Thy love.
Take my feet, and let them be swift
and beautiful for Thee.

Take my voice, and let me sing
always, only, for my King.
Take my lips, and let them be
filled with messages from Thee.
Take my silver and my gold;
not a mite would I withhold.
Take my intellect, and use
every power as Thou shalt choose.

Take my will, and make it Thine;
it shall be no longer mine.
Take my heart, it is Thine own;
it shall be Thy royal throne.
Take my love, my Lord, I pour
at Thy feet its treasure store.
Take myself, and I will be
ever, only, all for Thee.

—**Frances Havergal**

Alternate Hymn

When I Survey the Wondrous Cross

When I survey the wondrous cross
On which the Prince of glory died,
My richest gain I count but loss,
And pour contempt on all my pride.

Forbid it, Lord, that I should boast,
Save in the death of Christ my God;
All the vain things that charm me most,
I sacrifice them to His blood.

See, from His head, His hands, His feet,
Sorrow and love flow mingled down—
Did e'er such love and sorrow meet,
Or thorns compose so rich a crown?

Were the whole realm of nature mine,
That were an offering far too small;
Love so amazing, so divine,
Demands my soul, my life, my all.

—**Isaac Watts**

CHAPTER FOUR

Learning From Our Losses

Grief is far more than the feelings following the death of a loved one. Here we recognize the wide variety of unidentified losses and begin to grieve them—an important step toward living abundantly.

The slender puppy watched from across the busy road, tail wagging his entire rust-colored body. Finally, unable to restrain himself, he raced across the street to see why this odd assortment of people kept hauling belongings out of cars and vans and into the house.

Greeting the children, inspecting the boxes, sniffing the spring grass, his *joie de vivre* spread to us. We laughed and joked in the midst of heavy emotional work. Then, curiosity satisfied, the pup raced back across the road, almost as if he wanted to bring some good report to others. He never saw the speeding luxury van. "No!" my scream escaped just as the dog's body wedged under the tire. A horrified father braked, the wife clutched her husband's arm, children cried from inside the van.

Meanwhile, I unfroze from the front door of my friend's house, ran through the wide sweep of lawn, and across the highway. Tears poured down my cheeks as I shrieked at the driver, "Back up! You're crushing his leg." I knelt by the road, stroked the velvet ear, murmured to the dog. His terrified breathing slowed, his deep brown eyes searching mine. He appeared comforted by my touch and my words. Using a broom, someone pulled the puppy from under the van, and the driver, full of apologies to us and to his still-weeping children, drove off.

I crouched by the roadside until the squad car came. My tears did not stop when the police arrived; the puppy barely yelped at the muffled shot. "Couldn't be saved," the officer growled, shaking his head. But a dam had opened in my soul, and finally I left, unable to finish helping my friend with her move. *Where did such a waterfall of tears begin?* I asked myself as I drove the short distance home. *All this for a puppy you didn't even know?* Safe in our garage, the keening continued, and Rich came out to see where I was. He held me, bewildered, while I watered his flannel shirt.

The crying persisted intermittently throughout the day. The children were anxious and white-faced, wondering what was wrong with Mommy. My head pounded from the pressure of the tears. I did not know why I cried, but knew something important was happening within, some deep cleansing of wounds long ignored.

Months later I awakened in the night and began journaling about the incident. The puppy in his playful, happy curiosity represented all that was innocent, and lost, in my life. My life had been far from innocent, and I had forgotten how to play. I learned that life was serious, and dangerous, and playing should be relegated to the sandbox years and then left behind.

At the time of the puppy's misadventure, I was helping a friend whose husband chose rage and violence as his emotional response to life. She and her children were moving to a safe place. They, too, were finding life neither safe nor playful.

Another friend had buried her father after his long bout with brain cancer. Together, we had prayed for him, watching the Lord bring remission. But after the reprieve, the cancer, ugly and tenacious, eventually won the battle.

All this pain seemed to confirm the anguish of my early lessons: that living was hard, pain inevitable, and always the innocent seemed to suffer. That life should be smashed out of the puppy, frightened out of a child, stolen from a man with such a deep love for his family was too much to bear. Multiple losses combined in some reservoir under the surface, finally forming a pool large enough to capture my attention.

My mother-in-law tells the story of a man who developed problems with the foundation of his house. Digging around the outside, he unearthed some old clay drainage tiles. He dragged them to the side yard, buried them, and forgot them.

Until one day the yard exploded, turning into a fountain spewing dirt and grass and roots and clumps of soil. Evidently, the tiles pulled the underground moisture until so much pressure built up that the ground exploded.

This is hydrostatic pressure. Does burying our grief have the same effect eventually? Does something implode, spewing dirt and pain across the lawns of our lives? It felt as though someone had buried drainage tiles within my soul, forgetting to warn me that one day they might rupture and I would be ravaged.

Society trains us to bury our grief. Death is something to be avoided if at all possible. It is rare to sit at loved ones' bedsides, chaperoning them to the great divide. We no longer set the coffin in the front room, standing watch, allowing our children to play alongside the box of death.

"In Jewish tradition, persons in mourning were required to tear their clothes as an outward sign of grief," writes Elsie Neufeld.[1] "They were never to discard or exchange their apparel for a new outfit. But after a time they were allowed to mend the tears. The repaired seams had to be worn inside out, however, so all could see the frayed edges, the damage done by grief.

"There was good in that tradition. Our society discourages displaying grief. Even the once traditional black 'widow's clothing' is gone. The message is clear: Hide your pain."

Shades of Grief

Perhaps one of the problems we face is our narrowed definition of grief: mourning the death of another. For surely grief involves far more than physical loss of life. Grief is about other losses, as well: dreams, bodily function, roles, relationships, and unfulfilled expectations of those relationships.

And grief is more than that. One women's group cited other ways they experienced loss in their lives. Moving, divorce, death, retirement, unemployment, and the empty nest began the list. Others included the loss of innocence, loss of youth, loss of childhood, the marriage of a child, changes in an older parent, and improper parenting. Having less than an ideal marriage, being less maternal than we dreamed, the inability to conceive or bear children: all carry an unending grief.

A dear friend in an assisted living center, knowing she would never return to the house she and her husband built stone by stone, sold her home. Surely this is an occasion for deep grief. A woman whose home burned mentioned the loss of material things, such as photo albums and special mementos. Another suggested the intense and often unexpected grief following an abortion.

After living with and caring for an Alzheimer's patient for fifteen months, I wept over an article about former President Reagan. Nancy, his wife, mentioned her pain at the loss of sharing: she had the memories, but he could no longer reminisce with her. What an ache, having the loved one but not the mutual history.

After one seminar, the women divided into small groups to discuss some questions. Above the buzz of female voices the wrenching sound of sobbing could be heard. Not quiet weeping, but enormous, breath-catching cries. Later, tears poured down the face of one woman and anguished words from her lips. She sat still as stone, talking robotically while the pain gushed and streamed.

"I never knew. I never knew what this sadness, this short-temperedness, this anger was all about. I never looked at my life, really looked." Louise told of emotional isolation, neglect, the punishment received when she disobeyed, the creativity and joy snuffed out of her by authoritarian parents. She didn't realize what she'd missed because of their lack of parental love. And she didn't know how her family of origin's script had been directing her own parenting as a result. It occurred to me that rending one's clothing would be an appropriate outlet for the desperate energy that comes with mourning one's losses.

Learning to Listen to the Losses

Grief is a compounding of many losses, and our awareness of those losses comes in different ways. At times I have said, "I need a good movie to cry through, so I can get in touch with my pain." At other times, the intensity of my tears after a movie surprised me, clueing me in to an important loss, much like a small child tugging on her mother's skirt, begging for attention.

When tears pricked my eyes at seemingly innocuous moments, I blinked them away, annoyed. Finally, however, I started tracking these mini-weeps, trying to understand them. Was there a pattern—some subject that touched off the tears; an attitude from someone else; a common time of day, month, or year? Those salty tears began to bear the imprint of God's messages to me.

During a particularly weepy time, I apologized to Rich. "I don't even
know why I'm crying anymore. I can't seem to get to the bottom of this
well." At the time, boxes of belongings still lined the walls of our home
after a move. The deaths of my grandparents, six weeks apart, battered
against the feeble barrier I erected after moving. Drawing me into his
arms, Rich said, "Jane, you need to unpack your grief."

And so began the journey through my losses.

A Journey Begins With Just One Step

Listening to the tears, the next step in that journey was to contact a
nearby retreat house. I asked specifically for someone to guide me through
the retreat. It was ironic that others called it a retreat, because it was really
an advance—an advance on the past. I went, determined not to wallow
and regress but to move forward, to look loss in the face, to uncover this
grief that blanketed me in the form of depression and exhaustion.

No one told me what happens when we ignore our losses, when we
bury them, hide them in some dark place, and shut the door. Bolt it. But
I wondered as I hobbled around, nearly lame from ignoring the long-
repressed groaning of my soul, if we don't do other people a disservice by
not mourning our own losses.

For surely I was crippled, emotionally anesthetized, unable to feel either pain or joy. Only the darkness descended, almost daily, as I suc-
cumbed once again to the depression, a dark, black void, a rent in space,
a fracture in my frail psyche. And my family, living with a woman who
showed so little joy, walked carefully around me, anxious about any mis-
step that would upset the precarious balance of our lives.

The Scriptures assure us that weeping endures for a night, but joy
comes in the morning. Oh, for a taste of that joy! I keep walking. The long
journey is not yet over.

Grief's Timetable

"It seems there is no end to the grief. Deep, deep pools of it, reaching
far into my heart, washing over me unexpectedly in waves. Grief breaks
and crashes over my body, breakers rolling and foaming on the shoreline,
dribbling out to tiny fingers of water. Bubbles appear. A tiny sand creature
follows, only to be picked up mercilessly by the next pounding, crashing
wave. The creature never gains, only loses ground."

Those words, excerpted from my journal, remind me that grief has no orderly manner of appearing and disappearing. In spite of the stages of grief psychologists catalog, grieving is like the tide—in and out of tears, in and out of apathy, in and out of nightmares, in and out of pain.

When Frances lost her baby, the slow pace of healing discouraged her. She cried at my dining-room table, huge sobs racking her body. "It's been a whole month. I should be better."

Words seemed useless, so I knelt beside her chair, holding her. Finally, drawing a deep breath, my friend said, "Daniel thinks it's time for me to get on with my life, to set some goals, pick myself up, get back on track. But here I am, flat out on my back, crying. I feel so guilty. I'm doing nothing for the church right now."

Since when does God have a cutoff date for grief? Does the envelope read: "Warning: time-sensitive material. Discard by such and such a date"? Should we finish mourning a beloved member of our family in thirty days? How important was that person, if we miss him or her for only a month? Perhaps the best place for us to be is flat on our backs before God. He is far more interested in deepening our relationship with Him through the grieving process than in our attempts to earn His favor by our activities.

Playing Frisbee in the water on the ocean once, Rich and I didn't realize the journey the waves were leading us on. Every time the water caught the disk, the sea carried it a little farther down the shore, like a gleeful child running away with a treasure. When we looked up, we were hundreds of yards from our original location.

Grief is like that. We move in and out through the intensity of the crash and crawl cycles of the waves and feel as if we're making no progress. But one day we take stock of our surroundings and realize how far we've come from where we began.

Companions in the Grieving Process

How often my heart echoes the psalmist's cry, "You have taken my companions and loved ones from me; the darkness is my closest friend" (Ps. 88:18, NIV). Loss and grief are great isolators but also common denominators among all people.

Like most difficult processes, isolation during grief only intensifies the pain. Even Jesus, on the hardest road He would ever walk, "took with Him Peter and the two sons of Zebedee, and began to be grieved and distressed. Then He said to them, 'My soul is deeply grieved, to the point of death; remain here and keep watch with Me' " (Matt. 26:37–38).

Unfortunately, many fear the walk through another's valleys. C. S. Lewis wrote, "An odd by-product of my loss is that I'm aware of being an embarrassment to everyone I meet. At work, at the club, in the street, I see people, as they approach me, trying to make up their minds whether they'll 'say something about it' or not."[2]

"I'm still afraid of meeting those who have gone through tragedy," wrote Wilma Derkson.[3] "I think it's because they remind me of my own pain and refresh it."

Though we tend to keep our grief private, for true healing we need to share the pain, help others understand how we feel, and let them know what they can expect.

Mary Magdalene: A Model of Grieving

This past year swept me into Jesus' relationships with women. Remarkably, thirteen passages of Scripture mention Mary Magdalene, more than any other woman in His ministry group. Though we meet Mary Magdalene earlier in the Gospels, one of her most memorable recorded interactions with Jesus is at the gaping hole of death.

In John 20:1 we find Mary at the tomb. Darkness covers the land like a mantle of grief, and she creeps silently through the dew-wet garden. The entire earth is hushed in the predawn hours; the only sound may well have been that of her weeping.

According to John, Mary is the first to visit. Perhaps because her experience with Jesus—the deliverance from the seven demons—was so dramatic. Her Lord's shameful death ("cursed is anyone who hangs on a tree") possibly denied His followers the extensive and elaborate mourning expected in those days: professional mourners saving their tears in bottles, flutists and other musicians, a procession of weeping loved ones, days and days of remembering and laughing and crying, of honoring both the memory of the beloved and the grieving process.

Mary goes to the tomb to tend to the body, to make final preparations for burial. Because of the Sabbath, everything was temporary. She comes for the finality. Her tears must plunge from her cheeks, streak her garments, dampen the garden. Once set free from multiple demons, she must face one more: death.

Mary is a brave woman. While the disciples cower behind locked doors, she faces that which has hurt her the most: the horrific cave that now houses all that remains of the One who gave her life.

Imagine as she draws near to the tomb, worrying about the huge rock covering its mouth. Her mind is divided with the pain of loss and the practicalities before her: how will she move that stone? How will she get inside to care for her Lord's body?

But the stone is not there, nor the body of her beloved friend. The grief and anguish must well up, like Old Faithful ready to reassert its presence. Her grief has come here to rest, and she finds the tomb empty. Turning, Mary Magdalene is face-to-face with a man, a man she knows well but doesn't recognize.

In the turnaround time, Mary quickly goes through the stages of grief. In the throes of tears, she acknowledges her loss, feeling the pain. She then changes her relationship with the person who was lost: Jesus says, "Do not hold on to me." Next, she must decide how to grow from her loss, and in so doing, finds new meaning in her life. "And Mary of Magdala went to the disciples with the news: 'I have seen the Lord!' " (John 20:18, NIV). As a result of coming face-to-face with her loss, Mary becomes the first evangelist.

Grief's Harvest

Perhaps we can learn to honor the tears. In *Glittering Images*, an Anglican priest, overcome by grief at confession, said, " 'I must be mad because I can't stop crying and men never cry unless they're off their heads.' " His spiritual director countered with, " 'That's a very powerful myth in our culture and a myth which can produce extremely unhealthy results. Which is better: to express grief and pain by using tear-ducts especially created for the purpose or to express grief and pain by enduring a silent secret hemorrhage of the soul?' "[4]

Perhaps, remembering the tear bottles into which the professional mourners wept, we will begin to understand the depth of God's sorrow over our losses. The psalmist gives us a picture of the honor God accords our tears: "Put my tears in Thy bottle; are they not in Thy book?" (Ps. 56:8).

Perhaps, like Mary, when we look into the black, gaping mouth of grief and loss, we will turn. And turning, we will be embraced by a garden of beauty in the presence of the Gardener, the only One able to harvest joy from the seeds of our losses.

Quotes for Contemplation ————————————

On our way to Lazarus' tomb we stumble on still another question.
Jesus approaches the gravesite with the full assurance that he will raise his

friend from the dead. Why then does the sight of the tomb trouble him?

Maybe the tomb in the garden is too graphic a reminder of Eden gone to seed. Of Paradise lost. And of the cold, dark tomb he would have to enter to regain it.

In any case, it is remarkable that our plight could trouble his spirit; that our pain could summon his tears.

The raising of Lazarus is the most daring and dramatic of all the Savior's healings. He courageously went into a den where hostility raged against him to snatch a friend from the jaws of death.

It was an incredible moment.

It revealed that Jesus was who he said he was—the resurrection and the life. But it revealed something else.

The tears of God.

And who's to say which is more incredible—a man who raises the dead . . . or a God who weeps?"

> **—KEN GIRE,**
> **INCREDIBLE MOMENTS WITH THE**
> **SAVIOR**

The soul would have no rainbow had the eyes no tears.

> **—JOHN VANCE CHENEY,**
> **QUOTED IN DANCING IN THE DARK**

I believe God screamed when [my brother] John died. Loudly. No, not in thunder or in earthquakes, but through me, through the voice I woke to in the days following John's death. And in the voices of all who cried then and still cry for John. Isn't it logical that a God who comforts us through people would also cry through us?

> **—ELSIE NEUFELD,**
> **DANCING IN THE DARK**

One of the great benefits to entering into one's grief, pain and loss is the ability to fully experience joy and abundant life after the mourning.

> **—JANE A. RUBIETTA**

I think of the events surrounding Christ's death. The Bible tells us that darkness descended on the earth, the curtain in the temple ripped open, and an earthquake shook the land. Some interpret these events as symbols of a new era, an age when the temple and sacrifices were no longer required.

I think something deeper happened. I believe the events surrounding Christ's death were God's audible grief, translated into a language we could see and hear.

Who can deny the power of an electrical storm or an earthquake? God screamed when Christ died. God didn't want Christ to die, but there was no other way. *Christ prayed for another way: "My Father, if it is possible, may this cup be taken from me. Yet not as I will, but as you will" (Matt. 26:39, NIV). Isn't that a prayer spoken for all who mourn today? And isn't God's response then also God's response now? God doesn't want people to die. But there is no other way! Christ died at humanity's hand (the people chose!) and now too, people die at the hands of others.*

—**ELSIE NEUFELD,**
DANCING IN THE DARK

You need to claim the events of your life to make yourself yours.

—**ANNE WILSON-SCHAEF**

Before we bid goodbye to those present at the cross, I have one more introduction to make. . . .

There was one group in attendance that day whose role was critical. They didn't speak much, but they were there. Few noticed them, but that's not surprising. Their very nature is so silent they are often overlooked. In fact, the gospel writers scarcely give them a reference. But we know they were there. They had to be. They had a job to do.

Yes, this representation did much more than witness the divine drama; they expressed it. They captured it. They displayed the despair of Peter; they betrayed the guilt of Pilate and unveiled the anguish of Judas. They transmitted John's confusion and translated Mary's compassion.

Their prime role, however, was with that of the Messiah. With utter delicacy and tenderness, they offered relief to his pain and expression to his yearning.

Who am I describing? You may be surprised.

Tears.

Those tiny drops of humanity. Those round, wet balls of fluid that tumble from our eyes, creep down our cheeks, and splash on the floor of our hearts. They were there that day. They are always present at such times. They should be; that's their job. They are miniature messengers; on call twenty-four hours a day to substitute for crippled words. They drip, drop, and pour from the corner of our souls, carrying with them the deepest emotions we possess. They tumble down our faces with announcements that range from the most blissful joy to darkest despair.

The principle is simple; when words are most empty, tears are most apt.

—MAX LUCADO,
NO WONDER THEY CALL HIM
SAVIOR

Scriptures for Meditation

"Truly, truly, I say to you . . . you will be sorrowful, but your sorrow will be turned to joy. Whenever a woman is in travail she has sorrow, because her hour has come; but when she gives birth to a child, she remembers the anguish no more, for joy that a child has been born into the world. Therefore you too now have sorrow; but I will see you again, and your heart will rejoice, and no one takes your joy away from you."

—JOHN 16:20–22

The Spirit helps us in our weakness. We do not know what we ought to pray, but the Spirit himself intercedes for us with groans that words cannot express.

—ROMANS 8:26, NIV

He was . . . a man of sorrows,
and acquainted with grief. . . .
Surely our griefs He Himself bore,
And our sorrows He carried.

—ISAIAH 53:3–4

Those who sow in tears will reap with songs of joy.
He who goes out weeping, carrying seed to sow,
will return with songs of joy,
carrying sheaves with him.

—PSALM 126:5–6, NIV

Thou hast turned for me my mourning into dancing;
Thou hast loosed my sackcloth
and girded me with gladness;
That my soul may sing praise to Thee, and not be silent.
O Lord my God, I will give thanks to Thee forever.

—PSALM 30:11–12

"Your sun will set no more,
Neither will your moon wane;
For you will have the Lord for an everlasting light,
And the days of your mourning will be finished."
—ISAIAH 60:20

Journaling

This is a good time to visit your silent confidante, your journal. What feelings has the topic of loss stirred within? Move them to the outside of your mind by putting them in writing. Perhaps now you could journal about a specific memory of grief that comes to mind. Setting loss on a page externalizes it, much like exhaling frees our body of toxins.

Prayers of Confession, Praise, Petition

"Draw near to God and He will draw near to you," urges James (4:8).

Through the acts of confession and praise, cultivate the precious relationship you have with your Father in heaven. He longs to be near. Allow the Holy Spirit to reveal areas of neglect or sin.

Praise, logical in the aftermath of confession, is our time for communicating our love for God. Perhaps you could incorporate the praise portion into a walk (or a sit); under the skies, or below the stars. Praise is a natural response to forgiveness and creation.

Petition, then, the Lord of the universe regarding those needs and losses that you feel so keenly.

Moments for Creation

Grab some running shoes, or jump on your bike, and be exhilarated by God's created order. Try to focus your mind on what's happening outside. While loss is evident all around—fallen trees, dying flowers—so is renewal.

Silence

Move into a time of silence. After appreciating what's outside, invite the Lord to speak to you inside the recesses of your soul. The God who redeems our losses waits, longing to converse with you. In the silence, what does He impress upon your soul today? You may want to make note of these impressions after ending the time of silence.

Questions for Reflection ———————————

1. Construct a time line, or a history, of losses you've experienced. List those losses, your age and your response at the time of loss. Did you cry? Pray? Scream? Bury? Ignore? Withdraw? Why?

2. How did your family of origin deal with loss? What spoken and unspoken messages have you received about coping with grief? What messages have you passed on to your family about grief and loss?

3. In the next few weeks, notice occasions that trigger feelings of loss or grief, how you feel cheated when observing others' lives. Pay attention to anger: unreasonable anger may be a sign of grief.

4. The absence of mourning clothes and the limited definition of grief put the burden of communication about our losses and griefs on us alone. Our words notify others of our grief. What important people need to be made aware of the losses with which you are dealing?

5. "Blessed are those who mourn, for they shall be comforted," says Jesus in Matthew 5:4. Who will embody the comfort of our Lord for you as you face and grieve the losses of your life? Who do you need to draw into the circle of grief? What is it you want them to do for you?

6. Consider an affirmation about grief, and how you will handle future loss. For example, "Grief is a natural and healthy reaction. I will allow myself freedom and time to fully grieve this loss."

Hymn of Praise

WHAT A FRIEND WE HAVE IN JESUS

What a friend we have in Jesus,
All our sins and griefs to bear.
What a privilege to carry
Everything to God in prayer!

Oh, what peace we often forfeit,
Oh, what needless pain we bear,
All because we do not carry
Everything to God in prayer.

Have we trials and temptations?
Is there trouble anywhere?
We should never be discouraged;
Take it to the Lord in prayer.

Can we find a friend so faithful
Who will all our sorrows share?
Jesus knows our every weakness;
Take it to the Lord in prayer.

Are we weak and heavy laden,
Cumbered with a load of care?
Precious Savior, still our refuge;
Take it to the Lord in prayer.

Do thy friends despise, forsake thee?
Take it to the Lord in prayer!
In His arms He'll take and shield thee;
Thou wilt find a solace there.

—**JOSEPH M. SCRIVEN**

CHAPTER FIVE

Unforgiveness: The Bind That Ties

*Unforgiveness is a death in our souls. In this
chapter we learn to localize unforgiveness, call
it by name, see its symptoms and the
destruction it wields like a wrecking ball.*

At the sound of the crash, Emily leapt from bed. Nose pressed to her bedroom window, the five-year-old screamed, crying with the horror of a child who hadn't yet learned to hide fear under a layer of passivity. Terror filled her, sending her heart pounding through her body. Below her bedroom, outside the front door, her father stood bleeding, glass from a liquor bottle glistening with the blood in the moonlight. Emily's mother gripped the neck of the bottle, shouting in incoherent, drunken rage.

Every night for the remainder of her childhood, Emily would remember that scene, hear the shattering of glass, see the blood shining. Reinforced by other rages, different injuries, the horror became a subtle foundation for a life of withdrawal. Slowly, horror turned to resentment, and resentment to unforgiveness for the one who stole her childhood. Emily buried these seething emotions under a crippling layer of unfeeling.

Susan Lee, a dancer who was brutally raped, describes not her feelings after the violence but unforgiveness: ". . . frozen anger coiled in bitterness and resentment. It is as stifling as a muffled scream, a voiceless cry. It is an awesome feeling of helplessness and hurt, a trapped feeling worse than death itself."[1]

Unforgiveness is the bind that ties—chokes and contorts, poisons and paralyzes. Unforgiveness becomes a shield that states, "Anger protects me from any hurt another can inflict." Because nothing can make us forgive, unforgiveness helps compensate for the powerlessness of being hurt. It reminds us in a deadly whisper that we're the good guys, the real victims, the people injured by the bad guys.

With unforgiveness as our protector, we become emotionally challenged people, numb to other feelings. At thirty-five, with a husband and four children, Shayna found herself devoid of love, of joy, of laughter. Her principal emotion was broiling anger at everyone who interrupted her personal and professional goals. People were an inconvenience, an obligation.

Other symptoms of hidden unforgiveness are depression, energy loss, and loss of creativity. Low self-esteem, resentment, and underachieving may follow. Unforgiveness destroys our trust, our relationships, our home life, and our serenity.

As in many homes, "I'm sorry" and "That's okay" were common phrases in our family growing up. I was twenty-three and a newlywed when Rich met my apology with, "I forgive you." Hearing those words, I felt showered in warmth and understood what the Scriptures meant about a blessing being like warm oil. A deep awareness of how little I deserved such unqualified forgiveness swept over me; in seconds, forgiveness bridged the ravine I had created in our marriage.

Refusing to forgive is like pulling a blackout curtain over the soul. We cannot live without light. We can no longer allow the past to victimize us— whether the past is this morning, last year, or half a century ago. *Pre-forgiveness* is the first step.

Pre-Forgiveness

In the first stage of pre-forgiveness, we become willing to look into the gnarled, bitter face of unforgiveness, ready to acknowledge its cost. Our automatic "That's okay" response to others must cease. In pre-forgiveness we break the silence within ourselves and between us and our God.

In her book *Silent Pain*, Kathy Olsen says, "This very silence, this reluctance to face the pain, separates us from the vital parts of our souls that have been damaged."[2] In pre-forgiveness, we stop pushing the pain into what Olsen calls "the already bulging drawer of neglected emotions."

After this emotional reckoning, it's vital to notice how past pain hinders us now, hurting our relationships. This is the second stage of our pre-forgiveness journey.

For me, stasis is not comfortable; what's the point in being on a boat on a placid body of water? This became clear early in my marriage. Believing that a good wife did not create waves, I pushed down minor irritations and silenced my assumptions about my husband's behavior. All the while, unforgiveness rumbled like an underwater volcano. After too many weeks—or days—of closeness and unruffled waters, I employed a technique I call "create-a-crisis": pick something, anything, however minute, and blow it out of proportion. This catapulted me back into a comfortable, familiar milieu: a storm at sea. Probably not the best prescription for marriages of any age.

For Jenna, unforgiveness created mistrust, throwing instant walls between herself and others. She dated the same man for six years before becoming engaged; the engagement period lasted two more. The marriage endured eighteen months before her inability to trust destroyed any possibility for intimacy.

Unresolved pain from Marla's youth resulted in seeking intimacy where her heart and soul were uninvolved. Sexually active as a teenager, Marla birthed two children while single, has since gone through one marriage, and is on her second.

These expired coping mechanisms—techniques that once kept us safe but now hurt us—have three things in common. Alcoholics Anonymous sums them up concisely: Don't Talk, Don't Trust, Don't Feel.

After taking an inventory of our current state, and of the ramifications of unforgiveness, we must be willing to walk into our pain. Like the third stage in pre-forgiveness, it is much like walking into a burning house to save a child. In this instance, we are the children.

While still in the create-a-crisis stage of our marriage—which I periodically revisit—I reached a point where I knew I either walked through the pain or walked out of our marriage. Seeking counsel from Betsy, a friend and a certified therapist, the anguish seeped from my soul. Betsy's words are engraved on my heart: "Pain is a doorway to hope."

Because we live in an independent, do-it-yourself society, the temptation is to walk through the doorway, to race into the burning house, by ourselves. This is a grave mistake. Community is vital to recovery of any sort, including sifting through the rubble of unforgiveness. The right community forces us into honesty, affirms our steps, and supports us in the pain. This support may come from our local church, a small group, a women's prayer team, a Christian counselor, or a self-help group using the Twelve-Step approach. Whatever the case, take someone's hand when walking through that door.

Julie's husband didn't understand her pain or her reluctance to seek healing. She came to me, breaking on the inside, with the question, "How do I make myself walk through that door?"

If you ask this question as well, consider: What are you afraid will happen if you go through the doorway of pain? What are the consequences of staying on the "safe" side, where unforgiveness coils like a cobra ready to strike? Where is the community you need for the journey through the pain into hope and restoration?

Forgiveness: Untying the Bind

If unforgiveness is the bind that ties, twists, and paralyzes, forgiveness releases, straightens, energizes.

Forgiveness is being "willing to bear the pain." In walking through the door and choosing to forgive, we face the pain head on. We may have to relive the pain to get to the other side. David Seamands' books *Healing for Damaged Emotions, Putting Away Childish Things,* and *Healing of Memories* are excellent resources for a deeper look at moving through the pain toward healing.

Making Forgiveness a Habit

Forgiveness must begin vertically, between ourselves and God. Realizing that forgiveness is God's idea, God's way of life, humbles us. The psalmist asks, "If you, God, kept records on wrongdoings, who would stand a chance? As it turns out, forgiveness is your habit, and that's why you're worshiped" (Ps. 130:3–4, The Message). Who is this God we worship? "For Thou, Lord, art good, and ready to forgive, and abundant in lovingkindness to all who call upon Thee" (Ps. 86:5).

Knowing first who God is, that it is His habit to forgive, puts us in the right place at the right time, where we can investigate our souls in the searchlight of the Spirit (Ps. 139:23–24). Step Four in the Twelve-Step program boldly states, "Make a searching and fearless moral inventory." Though quick to get snagged on another's wrongdoing, we are slow to notice the rough edges of our own souls. We cannot forgive others without first seeing, and grappling with, sin in ourselves. Until we taste God's deep forgiveness through Jesus Christ for our own sins, we are powerless to forgive others.

In vertical forgiveness, others' wrongs are put into perspective with our own, and the cross focuses the picture: Christ's atoning death covers *all* sins, large and small.

After self-examination, 1 John 1:9 becomes a healing poultice: "If we confess our sins, He is faithful and righteous to forgive us our sins and to cleanse us from all unrighteousness."

Filling ourselves with the overwhelming love and mercy of the Lord readies us to begin horizontal forgiveness: forgiveness between ourself and another.

"In prayer there is a connection between what God does and what you do. You can't get forgiveness from God, for instance, without also forgiving others. If you refuse to do your part, you cut yourself off from God's part" (Matt. 6:14–15, The Message).

Even knowing the mercy of forgiveness, recently I wrestled with cruelty from another. I knew forgiveness would be required; but the hurt cut so deeply. Shame started to wrap around me because of my delay in forgiving, until I remembered a Body Fact. After breaking a bone, the soft tissue around the injury balloons, making setting the break impossible. When I broke a bone in my foot, I waited for days until the swelling went down so that they could cast my foot, thus beginning the final healing process.

In forgiveness, I came to regard that time between the injury and the forgiveness as a time of healing as well, necessary to the overall process. Time was required to reduce the swelling of damaged tissue surrounding my heart-wound. Forgiveness, the setting of the bone, the realigning of heart and attitude and action, may need to wait until the heart-swelling is reduced.

How do we then forgive? Naming the sin, the offender, and the offense, we choose on the basis of Christ's action on our behalf and in His presence to forgive. This is a determination on our part, not a feeling. And it is a work of God.

Feelings and Forgiveness

Even so, after forgiving, feelings don't always fall into line. Love and acceptance don't always replace hurt and anger immediately. The only way I have found to effect an about-face in my feelings has been prayer. I don't mean the "O God, zap me with love for so-and-so" type of prayer.

Once early in the pastorate an innocuous-looking envelope appeared, addressed to Rich. The letter, seething with hatred for Rich and his ministry, ended with, "Satan came to this church when you did." We both recognized the handwriting, and though we never discussed the letter, I felt as if I'd been bitten by a viper. Venom poisoned my soul for weeks, months, until contaminating my marriage, my family, and my ministry. I didn't even like God very much right then.

One morning the Holy Spirit seemed to nudge me toward forgiveness. Out of sheer obedience I forgave this person, but my feelings didn't line up with my action. "Pray for this person," the Spirit pushed. Days passed. Finally I began to pray for this person's soul, family, marriage, and work. And as I prayed, tears began to run down my burning cheeks. After several days I could see this person without mentally going for the jugular. Eventually Christ's compassion for the one who attacked my husband washed out the hatred in my soul. Though these and other memories haven't fallen away with my pain and hatred, they have softened and dimmed.

When Unforgiveness Returns

"Hon, can you help put Ruthie to bed? Our company is due in half an hour, and I need to finish dinner. 'Grandma' is confused today. She's in her room." Exhaustion and depression linked hands to chain my spirit in some dungeon, and my voice showed the wear.

As a seminary family, we cared for an elderly woman afflicted with Alzheimer's disease. This night, wrapping me in a reassuring hug, Rich swept our baby into his arms and disappeared upstairs. Later, checking on progress, I climbed the steps as Grandma burst from her room, totally disoriented. She'd abandoned her wig, and her wild, stringy hair lent an impression of madness. Hearing Rich singing to Ruthie, she slammed open the bedroom door, talking loudly to them.

The chain inside my dungeon jerked. I raged into the room, dragging Grandma out by the arm. We hurled word bombs at one another, both of us defensive. Finally, Grandma roared, "Get out of my house!" I stormed out, returning only after our friends arrived.

Filled with shame, I avoided Grandma's eyes. After dinner, with the guests gone, I headed for the kitchen to clean up. Quickly she appeared at my side, grabbing a towel to dry.

"Oh, Grandma, it's been a long day. Why don't you sit down and visit while I finish up?"

"Oh, no! You're my dearest friend in the world!" Watery eyes dared me to differ. "You would never do anything to hurt me! I want to help you now." A smile brightened Grandma's lined face.

Silence bound my tongue as I remembered our torrent of words. Could Grandma have no recollection of our earlier conflict? Tears traced paths down my cheeks. Pulling my hands from the soap suds, I hugged her. The chains of exhaustion and depression dissolved.

A seveny-six-year-old woman had demonstrated God's loving forgiveness: He completely erases our sins from His mind, then comes alongside and declares us friends.

Even though God forgets after we forgive, sometimes we remember. When Satan haunts us with specters of past sins ("See how you blew it there? Not very Christian, are you?"), we reclaim forgiveness and blow away the images. "I, even I, am the one who wipes out your transgressions for My own sake; and I will not remember your sins" (Isa. 43:25).

Moving Past Forgiveness

"Forgiveness is hard when the problem still exists," stated Jennie. She's right. Because unforgiveness places a rock in our baggage, becoming heavier and larger with each step, we have to consider confronting the one who hurt us. Allowing someone to continue hurting us undermines the value God places on us.

We grow when we forgive. But taking forgiveness one step further and confronting another when they continue to harm us has two benefits. First, we grow by facing down our fear of confrontation and affirming our worth to ourselves and to another. Second, we offer another the opportunity to grow through our forgiveness and through the chance to change destructive behavior.

We cannot change that behavior, we cannot demand change or contrition, but Scripture is clear. (See Col. 3:13.) We must forgive, regardless of another's lack of response.

Sometimes, though, we simply cannot confront a person, even while knowing pain will continue to be inflicted upon us. In these instances, we can erect a "police line": "Do not cross." By setting emotional boundaries, we refuse to give another the power to hurt us. Nancy implements this strategy. Having recognized certain subjects that trigger verbal darts, she sets boundaries when around her mother. If her mother mentions Nancy's career, her parenting, or her belief in God, Nancy tactfully but firmly steers the conversation in another direction.

Journey Toward Joy

The story of the paralytic, dragged into Jesus' presence by determined friends, delights me. Jesus said to the bedfast man, " 'Take courage, My son, your sins are forgiven.' " After much hue and cry, Jesus said, " 'In order that you may know that the Son of Man has authority on earth to forgive sins'— then He said to the paralytic—'Rise, take up your bed, and go home.' "

Imagine the paralytic's tentative steps after receiving forgiveness, then the firmer strides, and finally, the joy that captures his spirit. He runs and leaps toward home, shouting with praise to God. And in light of his healing, others are drawn to praise and glorify God (Matt. 9:1–8).

After receiving forgiveness, after our paralyzed spirits are liberated, our steps toward joy are tentative, then firmer, finally becoming leaps of praise. And others, seeing, will believe in the power of the One who sets the captives free.

Quotes for Contemplation

When we refuse to forgive one who has wounded us, we are bound together in a duel armlock. In some way, this binding prevents us from receiving God's love, but it also hinders that same love from pouring into the heart of the one who caused us pain.

**—KAREN MAINS,
KEY TO A LOVING HEART**

It may be an infinitely less evil to murder a man than to refuse to forgive him. The former may be the act of a moment of passion: the latter is the heart's choice. It is spiritual murder, the worst, to hate, to brood over the feeling that excludes, that kills the image, the idea of the hated.

**—GEORGE MACDONALD,
CREATION IN CHRIST**

Perhaps the childhood traumas and disappointments we have lived through are the very instruments God is using to lift us from being ordinary, routine people to being extraordinarily gifted ones. Perhaps it's those very things that hurt us in the past that now enable us to reach out to others.

**—JOYCE LANDORF,
THE HIGH COST OF GROWING**

Nothing I do to punish another for hurting me brings me healing.

—JANE A. RUBIETTA

He who cannot forgive others destroys the bridge over which he himself must pass.

—GEORGE HERBERT

Never does the human soul appear so strong and noble as when it forgoes revenge and dares to forgive an injury.

—E. H. Chapin

A Christian will find it cheaper to pardon than to resent. Forgiveness saves the expense of anger, the cost of hatred, or the waste of spirits.

—Hannah Moore,
as quoted in
The High Cost of Growing

"Satum—he got no future. He only got the past to work on, so he torments folks with the past—all the bad past—so folks be forgetting what they supposed to remember. . . . The Bible says, 'Now is the day of salvation.' The Bible says, 'Forget the things of the past and press forward.' Jesus blots out the sin and buries it in the ocean. Thank you, Jesus!"

—Margaret Jensen,
Lena

But all the wickedness in the world which man may do or think is no more to the mercy of God than a live coal dropped in the sea.

—William Langland

The final stage of forgiveness is to give away a part of yourself— reaching out to others with love and acceptance. What one person does for another is what's going to ignite and impact a whole people. So get outside yourselves. And forgive.

—A man, falsely imprisoned,
who began a ministry with
other inmates while in jail;
Susan Lee, as quoted in The
Dancer

Scriptures for Meditation

When you were dead in your sins and in the uncircumcision of your sinful nature, God made you alive with Christ. He forgave us all our sins, having canceled the written code, with its regulations, that was against us and that stood opposed to us; he took it away, nailing it to the cross. And having disarmed the powers and authorities, he made a public spectacle of them, triumphing over them by the cross.

—Colossians 2:13–15, niv

*"I, even I, am the one who wipes out your transgressions for My own sake;
And I will not remember your sins."*

—ISAIAH 43:25

*He has not dealt with us according to our sins,
Nor rewarded us according to our iniquities.
For as high as the heavens are above the earth,
So great is His lovingkindness toward those who fear Him.
As far as the east is from the west,
So far has He removed our transgressions from us.*

—PSALM 103:10–12

*"Her sins, which are many, have been forgiven, for she loved much;
but he who is forgiven little, loves little."*

—LUKE 7:47

"Who is this man who even forgives sins?"

—LUKE 7:49

*And so, as those who have been chosen of God, holy and beloved, put on
a heart of compassion, kindness, humility, gentleness and patience; bearing
with one another, and forgiving each other, whoever has a complaint against
anyone; just as the Lord forgave you, so also should you. And beyond all
these things put on love, which is the perfect bond of unity.*

—COLOSSIANS 3:12–14

Journaling

Abraham Lincoln said, "It is indispensable to have a habit of observation
and reflection." Take some moments to observe your reactions to the above
writings: the introductory reading, the quotes for contemplation, and the
Scriptures. Reflect, in writing, places that engaged your emotions, or when
memories surfaced. Use your journal to debrief, to vent, to valve.

Prayers of Confession, Praise, Petition

During these next minutes, settle in before the Lord. Invite the Holy
Spirit to bring to the screen of your mind any areas where you have strayed
from Him. The wait can be time-consuming; be patient. Flow from confession into praise to the One who has brought you out of darkness into

His marvelous light. Finally, place before the Lord the people weighing heavily upon your heart, and then present your own needs.

Moments for Creation

Today you may want to combine time outside with a time of prayer. As you observe God's work on your behalf, let praise bubble forth. Deep breaths, working muscles, and an active heart surely make the Lord smile!

Silence

To begin the time of silence, reread one of the Scripture selections, or choose a favorite of your own. Meditate on an aspect of God's person, such as His incredible capacity to forgive. You might even choose a phrase, such as, "Forgiving Father," to focus your heart and thoughts.

After the time of silence, however brief or long, jot down in your journal the thoughts the Lord impressed upon your heart.

Questions for Reflection

1. What are you afraid will happen if you go through the door of pain toward healing and forgiveness? What are the consequences of staying on the "safe" side, unforgiveness coiling within like a cobra ready to strike? Where is the community you need for the journey through the pain into hope and restoration?

2. What survival techniques have you employed that are no longer helpful, but in fact damage you and your relationships? (For example, "Don't talk, don't trust, don't feel.") In what situations do you use them?

3. Of whom do you need to ask forgiveness? Why? Why have you waited to resolve the issue? How has being unreconciled affected you and your relationships? What is the Holy Spirit inviting you to do?

4. If you hold unforgiveness toward one who has died, consider writing that person a letter, explaining how past actions on his/her part hurt you. Empty the anger onto paper, and then in obedience envision him/her, and choose to forgive in Christ's name. Destroy the paper, symbolic of destroying the bondage of the memories, pain, and unforgiveness.

5. Imagine that the police are coming to investigate a robbery. Create a list of qualities stolen from you by the person in the past. For example, your innocence, your childhood, your ability to laugh. Create a second list of qualities that your own unforgiveness has stolen from you and from those you love. In the presence of Christ, claim the replacement of these qualities by the restorative power of the Holy Spirit. (See Is. 43:19; John 10:10.)

Hymn of Praise

FORGIVE OUR SINS AS WE FORGIVE

(To the tune of "Amazing Grace")

"Forgive our sins, as we forgive,"
You taught us, Lord, to pray;
But you alone can grant us grace
To live the words we say.

How can your pardon reach and bless
The unforgiving heart
That broods on wrongs and will not let
Old bitterness depart?

In blazing light your cross reveals
The truth we dimly knew:
What trivial debts are owed to us,
How great our debt to you!

Lord, cleanse the depths within our souls,
And bid resentment cease;
Then, bound to all in bonds of love,
Our lives will spread your peace.

—ROSAMOND E. HERKLOTS[3]

CHAPTER SIX

The Fertile Land of Emotions

"Keep the feelings on the outside," my friend advised. We tend to bury them—then burn everyone we come in contact with. Here we learn to direct our feelings either toward the Lord or toward someone we feel is responsible for invoking those feelings.

The farm rested on hundreds of acres of the most fertile land in Tennessee, with a driveway that seemed, to a child's mind, to wind and stretch endlessly through fluffy-topped fields of cotton. As an adult, I routed a return trip past the farm, which had long since passed out of family hands. Our three children bounced in the backseat, excited to see where Mommy spent happy weeks as a child. Stalks that once held bouquets of cotton stood at attention, crisp and rustling, in stark contrast to the surprising whiteness of snow on the ground. With the entire area frozen down in a freak ice storm, I wondered if we'd lost our collective minds.

We slipped and slid to a stop at the gate. I had never seen it closed. Rusty chains and signs shouted ominously, "No Trespassing!" "Private Drive!" "Keep Out!"

Turning in my seat, I eyed my husband. "Oh, well. Guess that's that."

Always ready to retreat at the least sign of difficulty, I compressed my lips and started to reverse the car. Rich's hand stopped me.

"Let me take a look."

While we waited in the car, travel weary, gritty, and edgy, he hopped out and challenged the gate—man to . . . steel. And won! Within minutes he wrenched off the lock and chains, tugging free the near-frozen blockade. Rich stood aside like a true gatekeeper, gesturing regally to let us pass.

Watching the hinges give way, I realized the scenario symbolized the gate, chain, and padlock barring the door to my heart, my passions, my feelings, and memories.

My husband has played an important part in empowering me to move beyond the self-imposed signs and warnings and barred gateways to my past and to my future. By his steady love and acceptance, he has taught me to pull, tug, and disregard the "no trespassing" warnings posted by this territorial landowner over my heart.

As we crunched down the mile-long driveway, Rich caught my hand in his. "You have every right to be here, Jane."

Tears and emotions crowded close to the surface. I nodded. Surrounded by sterile, frozen earth, I moved beyond the gates, aware that I entered emotionally uncharted territory. Little did I know that the stark land would begin to bloom with abundance and new life as my feelings thawed.

Emotional Roadblocks

For many women, multiple chains and gates bar access to our feelings. One barrier may be a sense of vulnerability. After a heartbreaking season of facing and sharing unknown feelings, Beth said, "I feel like a clock with all my insides hanging out."

Examining our emotions increases a sense of vulnerability. We may have to battle an instinctive shut-down reflex. In extremely cold weather, our bodies automatically telegraph our limbs, slowing down the blood flow, desensitizing our arms and legs. The message reads, "Preserve the center of life, the heart and brain, at all costs." Emotionally, I believe our hearts send involuntary messages as well: self-preservation regardless of the toll taken on our soul and our relationships. To feel means to be vulnerable, so we learn to function with the fear and keep the feelings frozen.

Accompanying this fear of vulnerability may be the dread that, if we air our deepest emotions, we won't be accepted and loved. One woman confessed, "I know my husband doesn't like my tears, so I do everything

I can to refrain from crying around him. I don't want to be accused of manipulating him through tears, but sometimes I need to be helped and allowed to cry." Unfortunately, this couple is missing out on one benefit of sharing the pain: intimacy which comes from weeping with those who weep, comforting those who mourn.

The frightening side of withholding our tears from our spouses is that someday, a man may come along who promises to meet those emotional needs. We must be faithful to do our emotional work at home and with trusted friends so we aren't tempted to go outside of morally acceptable avenues to get those needs met.

In the movie *Dead Man Walking*, Sean Penn portrayed a man on death row for a grisly double murder. He seemed incapable of experiencing and expressing grief, anguish, repentance. As I work with women, sometimes I wonder if we are dead women walking, automatons marching through our roles and responsibilities without regard to the underlying emotions.

Some underground message seems to have circulated among Christian women that neutrality in all emotions is imperative to living a holy life. It is as if some puritanical restriction demands that we keep down our feelings regardless of the cost to ourselves and our relationships. Did someone tell us that feelings are unspiritual, of the flesh, unbecoming to women of God? Are we afraid of being indulgent, weak-willed women whose every tear or chuckle leads to hysteria, afraid we'll walk around sobbing like professional wailing women or laughing like hyenas?

Perhaps behind our hesitation to be honest with our feelings is a past message regarding their inappropriateness. "There, there, don't cry." "Control yourself." "Calm down." Shush phrases may eventually silence our emotional expression.

One of the biggest roadblocks to our feelings may be misunderstanding the vital role emotions play in our lives.

Emotional Necessity

For years I pushed feelings to the extreme margins of my life, trying to ignore them if at all possible. Emotional numbness kept me from experiencing much pain. It also blocked not only my joy but my experiences of connection with others.

Genuine intimacy is impossible with feelings imprisoned behind lock and chain. True godliness is possible only when we become familiar with our interior landscape, understanding and working through our feelings in the presence of God. Emotions are a gift that can lead us into growth.

By exploring the world of feelings, we tap into a wealth of closeness with others and with God.

Feelings are messengers delivering valuable information. Only by looking at anger more deeply did I discover a new facet of this misunderstood emotion: for me, anger is rarely a pure, justice-related feeling. Jesus' anger in the temple is considered righteous anger. My own anger is rarely righteous in the pure, other-directed sense. Anger is often a signpost pointing to deeper feelings of insignificance. Perhaps another's words or actions made me feel unloved or worthless or unimportant.

Reading Scripture I see the psalmist's often overwhelming emotions. His bed swam with tears, he called curses on enemies, he danced jubilantly before God. No one could accuse David of severed feelings and emotional paralysis! The New Testament, likewise, is a picture of the body of Christ warmly enveloping believers in comfort, encouragement, and loving acceptance.

The Scriptures reveal a Jesus who wept at His friend's death; a God who grieves over His children; the Holy Spirit, the Comforter, who sweeps along beside us to hold us in our pain. And this God has a sense of humor. Surely God laughed at the first giraffe! Surely Jesus chuckled at His word pictures: a camel going through the eye of a needle! And surely our heavenly Father hoots at some of our antics, as a parent laughs at her child's immature missteps. As I look more deeply at my emotions, I realize God longs to hold me against His chest and let me burrow into His shoulder. I imagine my tears wetting His garment, my laughter lighting up His face, my joy filling His heart, and I know that feelings are intended to carry us straight into the arms of God.

Emotions are the gateway into growth, into God, and into deeper, trusting relationships that personify the love, grace, and acceptance of Jesus Christ.

Even so, life isn't meant to be an emotional free-for-all. There are healthy limits to the benefits of emotions.

Limits to Emotions

"Glad. Mad. Sad." The psychologist's simple words made sense. "Healthy children free-flow between these three emotions every day. Majoring on any particular emotion to the exclusion of the others is a signal that something is wrong."

As wives, parents, and friends, we look for this healthy balance in those we love. As women, we must look for the same balance in our own lives.

"Normal" is experiencing a broad range of feelings daily. The absence of joy signals dangerous contours of the shoreline beneath the water. We need to school ourselves to look below the water for the reasons.

If tears are our constant companions for too many days and nights, we must find out why. If we can't remember the last time we felt sad or angry, perilous emotions may be building up under the surface of our lives. If anger is the only sensation we come up with in the "Name That Feeling" game, it's time to dig deeper.

Waiting for Love

I grew up watching "The Fickle Finger of Fate Award" on prime-time television. I don't believe in fate, but of all emotions, love may be the most fickle. If couples based their decisions on whether they *felt* love, they'd be married and divorced daily. For many women, feelings of love fluctuate depending on hormone levels, sleep patterns, health, and spiritual consistency.

Assuming that the absence of loving feelings means that they will never return is dangerous. One woman, numb after years in a controlling marriage, stated, "I just don't love you anymore." As her husband began to change, a wise counselor suggested waiting out the feelings, watching for a return of the feeling of love. In the end, love is not so much a feeling as a commitment and an action.

Absence of love isn't the only feeling we can't trust either.

Horrifying Hormones

"I have a new word," I told my friend. "Hor-motion."

Hor-motions are the ones we can't trust. These are the feelings that threaten to capsize our ships (and all on board!) for a day or two every month, depending on the levels of hormones in our system. It's taken years, but finally when I begin to feel an overwhelming urge to cry or scream I look at the calendar and calculate. When I'm aware of my body's cycles, I know when it's a good time to deal with an issue and when it's better to postpone all conflict resolution until an even-keel day.

Part of our fear of emotions may be the power they exert. Learning to let the emotions lead us correctly is paramount.

Feelings as Tutors

As grand as emotions are, God never intended that our emotions lead us to hurt others. Rather, He desires that they bring us into closer relationships. Passion is meant to teach us about the depth of committed love, to help us enter into a land rich in relationship and trust; passion is not meant to destroy a committed relationship with an outside fling. "I am a jealous God," the Scriptures tell us. Our jealousy, like other emotions, is meant to teach us about the God who desires our company beyond all else.

A Word About Anger

For many, the most frightening emotion may be anger, because adrenaline surges accompany it. Prehistoric people, fighting for survival, required adrenaline surges for self-preservation. But what do we do with the energy surge? "Be angry, and yet do not sin," writes Paul to the Ephesians; too often anger becomes a wedge in relationships rather than a catapult springing us into greater intimacy.

Expressing anger in a way that is not damaging is tricky. One friend used her anger to carefully confront her employer. When that yielded no fruit beyond the value of expression, she asked, "How do I get rid of this anger?" One writer turned her anger into an award-winning essay on exclusion in the church.

Another way may be to burn away the adrenaline with something extremely physical. During one bout of anger, I ran up and down twelve flights of stairs rather than destroy property or someone's reputation (including mine).

Jogging, an aerobic workout, biking, or the treadmill are other ways to use up anger's energy. Rearranging furniture, chopping wood, and gardening are other possibilities. The cooling-off period is a good time to decide how much of the root of anger needs to be shared in key relationships.

Using Emotions

"There is no one," I sobbed at my desk. "No one I can talk to about my pain." I put my head down on my journal. Silence throbbed around me. In that stillness I sensed a waiting. In the shadows, like an actor anticipating His cue, the Lord stood with arms outstretched. In my isolation, I overlooked the One ready to enter the drama and enfold me in His embrace.

For all of my awareness of emotions, it takes painfully long to put into practice what I know. My reaction is to push the feelings underground, to burrow around like a mole hiding from the sun.

How can emotions be harnessed for maximum energy? Only by externalizing them, by sharing them in safe, appropriate relationships, by bringing them out of the darkness into the light. "Keep the feelings on the outside," my friend Lisa told me.

There are appropriate ways to express our feelings. Owning them is a good start. For instance, "I feel as if I'm the only one cleaning the house, and I feel angry about that," is a better approach than raging, "You are all lazy, self-indulgent slobs, and I don't care if you live like pigs anymore. I'm leaving the pigpen." Using the first example, we are not accusing others of anything, our voice is controlled, and we are not name calling. We own the anger rather than blaming the others for the anger. Then we can discuss accomplishing the work with a team approach.

Emotions can be radioactive waste burning our souls and charring our relationships, or they can be recycled into useable fuel for our lives. Emotions can silence us, hurt us (and/or others), or lead us through the gateway into deepening maturity.

The Usher

Are there bars, gates, chains, and warning signs over your heart? Perhaps you have no husband to usher you into the land of emotional growth; maybe you are not surrounded by spiritually and emotionally mature friends who can guide you into new territory.

But the Holy Spirit waits at the gate, ready to loosen the rusty chains and remove the padlocks, longing to usher us into not a land of frozen whiteness but a fertile land, rich and vibrant. A safe place. "You shall no longer be termed Forsaken, nor shall your land any more be termed Desolate; but you shall be called Hephzibah, and your land Beulah; for the Lord delights in you, and your land shall be married" (Isaiah 62:4, NKJV).

In the end, to enter is up to us.

Quotes for Contemplation ————————————————

Anger is often a clue to a deep personal need that is not being met. In many cases it is appropriate to be angry—at injustice, falsehood, cruelty. Jesus showed anger at the greed and materialism in His Father's house. Ask God to show you the root of your anger. Reflect on it in your journal until you understand it better.

—LUCI SHAW,
CAN I CONTROL MY CHANGING
EMOTIONS?

Love involves choice and commitment. Love is not only feelings. We may not always feel love, but if we make a choice to love and follow that with a commitment to love and honesty, with time the feelings will follow. Even then, we can expect our feelings of love to ebb and flow. And for that reason feelings cannot serve as the only benchmark to measure the quality of my relationships but, instead, my actions of love—my concern and willingness to meet another's needs. . . . To keep love from becoming an emotional roller coaster, learn to focus on the needs of those you love and how you can meet those needs rather than on how you "feel" about the person.

—LUCI SHAW,
CAN I CONTROL MY CHANGING
EMOTIONS?

"How are you?"
"GR-R-EAT! And how are you?"
"FAN-TAS-TIC! How's the work going?"
"GR-R-EAT! How about yours?"
"FAN-TAS-TIC!"
And everybody is so great and wonderful and super and colossal that you begin to wonder how anybody could possibly have taken time out for this [meeting]. And that's just great if you're doing great and that's fantastic if you're really doing fantastic, but lots of times they are just words that shield and hide because it's not easy to say you're doing just lousy when everybody else is so great. . . . And I often wonder how our . . . church gatherings would turn out and how far-reaching their results would be if someone would just have the courage to say: "I'm not great— I'm not fantastic—I'm so discouraged, I'm about to die and I need your prayers and love." . . . And I wonder, too, how the world would be changed if we didn't think it was a mark of strength . . . to keep from showing our feelings.

—BOB BENSON,
COME SHARE THE BEING

Feelings are never conjured intentionally. They originate independently and have a life of their own. It's important to name and acknowledge them when they do surface. Otherwise they begin to control the body they inhabit.

—ELSIE NEUFELD,
DANCING IN THE DARK

Anger touches on every aspect of our lives. . . . We know our greatest anger, as well as our deepest love, in our roles as daughters, sisters, lovers, wives, and mothers. Family relationships are the most influential in our lives, and the most difficult. It is here that closeness often leads to "stuckness," and our efforts to change things only lead to more of the same. When we can learn to use our anger energy to get unstuck in our closest and stickiest relationships, we will begin to move with greater clarity, control, and calm in every relationship we are in, be it with a friend, a co-worker, or the corner grocer. Issues that go unaddressed with members of our first family only fuel our fires in other relationships.

—**HARRIET GOLDHOR LERNER,**
THE DANCE OF ANGER

Emotional maturity is the ability to know what it is that I am feeling, what its name is, then to discover positive channels for it. The quicker the process operates in us, the more mature we are becoming. Spiritual maturity requires that we submit to this procedure before the Lord. . . . If Christian women have a common flaw, it is that we continually settle for being less than what God intends us to be. We desperately need examples of women who WERE not and ARE not content to be less than spiritually significant.

—**KAREN BURTON MAINS,**
KAREN KAREN

We all have important emotional issues—and if we don't process them up the generations, we are more than likely to pass them on down.

—**HARRIET GOLDHOR LERNER,**
THE DANCE OF INTIMACY

We can never attain to the full knowledge of God until we have first known our own soul thoroughly. Until our soul reaches its full development we can never be completely holy.

—**JULIAN OF NORWICH**

Scriptures for Meditation

I'm an open book to you; even from a distance, you know what I'm thinking. You know when I leave and when I get back; I'm never out of your sight. You know everything I'm going to say before I start the first sentence. I look behind me and you're there, then up ahead and you're

*there, too—your reassuring presence, coming and going. This is too much,
too wonderful—I can't take it all in!*

*Oh yes, you shaped me first inside, then out; you formed me in my
mother's womb. I thank you, High God—you're breathtaking! Body and
soul, I am marvelously made! I worship in adoration—what a creation!
You know me inside and out, you know every bone in my body; You know
exactly how I was made, bit by bit, how I was sculpted from nothing into
something.*

—**PSALM 139:2–6, 13–16,**
THE MESSAGE

*You will keep him in perfect peace,
Whose mind is stayed on You,
Because he trusts in You.*

—**ISAIAH 26:3,** NKJV

*Now may the God of hope fill you with all joy and peace in believing,
that you may abound in hope by the power of the Holy Spirit.*

—**ROMANS 15:13,** NKJV

*"When you pass through the waters, I will be with you;
And through the rivers, they shall not overflow you.
When you walk through the fire, you shall not be burned,
Nor shall the flame scorch you."*

—**ISAIAH 43:2,** NKJV

*For we do not have a High Priest who cannot sympathize with our
weaknesses, but was in all points tempted as we are, yet without sin.*

*Let us therefore come boldly to the throne of grace, that we may
obtain mercy and find grace to help in time of need.*

—**HEBREWS 4:15–16,** NKJV

*Protect me, O God, for in you I take refuge.
I say to the Lord, "You are my Lord;
I have no good apart from you. . . ."
I keep the Lord always before me;
because he is at my right hand, I shall not be moved.
Therefore my heart is glad,
and my soul rejoices; my body also rests secure.*

—**PSALM 16:1–2, 8–9,** NRSV

Journaling

Are there times when your emotions control you? Do feelings of shame surface when you remember those times? Ironically, when we are busy burying those feelings we have in fact turned over the reins of control to the feelings. Spend some time thinking about your general attitude toward emotions and their roles in your life. What messages have you received in the past about feelings? How did your mother display her emotions? How does your church approach feelings? What do you see in Scripture about feelings?

Prayers of Confession, Praise, Petition

Did some emotions boil up as you began to look below the surface? The only emotions separating us from God are those we do not express to Him. Bring these feelings into the presence of God; pour them out at His feet. God knows how we feel; He's not surprised by our passion, our anger, our pain, our joy. Turn now to that safe place in a time of prayer.

Moments for Creation

Deep breaths in our Father's world bring amazing peace and clarity. Without an agenda for this time, take a leisurely walk. Observe. Let the Lord sing to you through the wind in the trees; hear His voice in the babbling brook. Watch for His creative hand in the world. Let His peace sink into your soul. Be at rest.

Silence

Let the silence enfold you. Invite the Comforter to come, to make you aware of His presence. Rest there, safe, secure, accepted, loved. Listen for the whispers the Lord will plant in your heart.

Questions for Reflection

1. Who meets your emotional needs? With whom do you share your joy, your anger, your fear, your sadness? Where do you need to shore up the support? How can you take these relationships and craft them to better meet your emotional needs?

2. We cannot expect family members to meet our every emotional need. They may be part of our emotional network, but the network must extend beyond mates, parents, or siblings. How easy is it to go to God with your emotional needs?

3. How do you think God feels about your pain? Your anger? Your passion? Your joy?

4. What fears do you battle as you consider emotions and their expression? Quickly write down some of the messages you learned as a girl and as a teenager about feelings. Do you have a defense mechanism when it comes to your emotions? For instance, hiding anger behind sarcasm, or joking away sadness?

5. Have there been times when revealing your emotions backfired; or you ended up hurt; or you were rejected? Write down some of your feelings surrounding those times. Can you bring this package of pain into God's presence and weep with Him over it?

6. Occasionally, run through a "feeling check." Label the emotion running through you right now and look for the reasons behind it. This is good practice for daily life, for conflict resolution, for integrity in relationships.

7. Thinking about your life—is there an emotion missing? Joy? Love? Anger? In God's presence, begin to delve into that missing emotion, and see where He leads you.

8. Just for fun, check out Jack Kent's *There's No Such Thing as a Dragon* (Racine, Wis.: Western Publishing Co., 1975) from the children's section of your local library . Seen any dragons lately?

Hymn of Praise ————————————————

O LOVE THAT WILT NOT LET ME GO

O Love that wilt not let me go,
I rest my weary soul in Thee;
I give Thee back the life I owe,
That in Thine ocean depths its flow
May richer, fuller be.

O Light that followest all my way,
I yield my flickering torch to Thee;
My heart restores its borrowed ray,
That in Thy sunshine's blaze its day
May brighter, fairer be.

O Joy that seekest me through pain,
I cannot close my heart to Thee;
I trace the rainbow through the rain,
And feel the promise is not vain,
That morn shall tearless be.

O Cross that liftest up my head,
I dare not ask to fly from Thee;
I lay in dust life's glory dead,
And from the ground there blossoms red
Life that shall endless be.

—GEORGE MATHESON

CHAPTER SEVEN

In the Vise: Squeezing the Best Out of Stress

Stress is a fact of life. In most instances we cannot change our many stressors; we can only change the ways we deal with stress. In this retreat we will learn to identify and minimize stress reactions.

Circular and angry, the red blotch on my arm drew my attention, but I was busy and ignored it. The next day, the funny marks formed ridges on the outside, flattened on the inside, like miniature craters, and spread up my entire arm. Within a week they covered my arms and crawled up my legs. Each morning I peered anxiously in the mirror, fearing more than anything that these blemishes would creep up onto my face while I slept. This vanity made me realize that something was happening to my body that I didn't understand. My doctor referred me to a specialist, and I hied off to sort things out in a plush office with lots of fingerprint-free windows.

"Sometimes these types of spots indicate a reaction to a medication. What have you been taking?" asked the specialist.

I named an antibiotic I'd tried six months earlier, and which I was again using to treat a second round of sinusitis.

The doctor nodded; he'd been around. "Sometimes, of course, these things are the result of stress." He eyed me keenly.

I all but snorted and settled for rolling my eyes dramatically.

"Are you under stress right now?"

Crossing my legs, then uncrossing them because the plague was uncomfortable, my sigh worked its way up from my toes. My body betrayed me. I nodded. "Probably the most highly stressed time so far in my life."

"Do you sleep at night?"

"Like the dead." As an afterthought, I added, "When I finally get to bed."

"Do you anticipate an end to the stressors soon?"

I wondered, if I said no, if he would just put me into a nice hospital bed with a soft gown and have professionals bring me food, provide soothing counsel, and clean my room.

We flipped through my mental calendar. My agenda for the next three weeks included delivering new keynote addresses for a major women's conference; three batches of out-of-town company; packing up our family, our home, and two home-based businesses and moving ninety miles away; and all the accompanying transition trauma. This did not take into account two publishers awaiting more work on two separate books, which I blithely agreed to forward within six weeks. Nor did I look backward at the summer's many milestones, each of which was highly stressful.

In truth, the stressors would change, but they wouldn't end. After the move would come all the settling in and locating schools and doctors and beginning in a new church and finding new friends and grocery stores and trying to squeeze work into the tourniquet that was my life and then write the work so I could deliver the work and . . .

We agreed I would avoid that particular antibiotic, he prescribed something to combat a possible allergic reaction, and I left, wishing he'd shoved a plane ticket for Hawaii into my hands, canceled my summer plans, and ordered me to take a vacation.

After the move, the blotches eventually went away. One or two redden my skin occasionally, a reminder of how attuned our bodies are with our spirits and minds, a memento of the life that alternately weaves and howls around us like so much bad weather.

Stress

We have good stress and call it *eustress*. We have bad stress and it becomes *distress*. But with *no* stress, we're dead.

What, exactly, is stress? Is it life demanding more of us than we have to give? Stress does not exist apart from our interpretation of our lives. It is not some free agent, roaming around looking for a likely body to inhabit. Nor is stress pressure put on us from our lives.

Simply put, changes in life require changes in the way we live our lives; stress is the body's attempt to adjust to and deal with those changes. These changes may be external—our health, our home, our work, our relationships. Though less recognized, stress can be caused when changing ideas and perspectives force us to reexamine our values.

Roy M. Oswald extends our understanding of stress beyond such changes: "Stress exists wherever there is a lack of clarity about one's tasks or role or value."[1]

We might be tempted to define stress as "just being too busy." Busyness certainly intensifies our reactions, but I'm beginning to wonder if stress is rooted, not in busyness, but in the fact that our intense schedules isolate us from ourselves, from our God, and from our relationships. Perhaps the problem isn't busyness, but isolation. Not ALONE-ness, but that critical separation from our souls and from the heart and voice of God.

Health Havoc

This separation exacts a costly toll on our health. A number of stress-related problems exist, such as high blood pressure, ulcers, and heart disease. An increase in general aches and pains, headache, lower back pain, and muscle spasms have been attributed to stress. Stress has been linked to psycholosocial problems: substance abuse, depression, and sleeping and eating disorders. Poor eating and sleeping habits wreak havoc on our health as well, further eroding our stress-resiliency.

Our bodies have a physiological reaction to stress, beginning with a demand for adrenaline, which increases our susceptibility to related health problems. The week before a large speaking engagement, as I prepare my talks, I begin to dip into the reservoir of adrenaline. Speaking before a group further taps my reserves, requiring huge amounts to give me the necessary push. More adrenaline drains out after the talk, when I speak one on one with women. By the time I get to my car or the airplane, the rush from speaking has evaporated, like dew in the desert. Old Mother Hubbard's cupboards are bare, my larder depleted, and I wonder if I can make it home. It may take days to replenish that reservoir. If more adrenaline is demanded before my system recuperates, I'm exceedingly vulnerable to stress and its toll, a toll ultimately exacted on my family and my soul.

These reservoirs of adrenaline are finite and must be refilled. Make too frequent demands on the body for more adrenaline to see us through crisis after crisis, and our physical, mental, and spiritual capabilities wear thin at the edges. Adrenaline was meant to be fuel for our bodies in an emergency flight-or-fight situation. Unfortunately, we have become adrenaline-dependent, addicted to living on the rush.

Rate Yourselves

When a friend attended a stress workshop as part of a writer's conference, she was stunned to receive an award for racking up the most stress points in her class. The gift? A book to give to her family on how to plan her funeral. Learning about the body's limited capacity to deal with change has helped Lynn to better manage her life. It's interesting to note that our bodies interpret even pleasant, positive events as stress.

Which of the following have occurred in your life during this year? Add up the point values of each.

Value	Event
100	Death of spouse
65	Marital separation
63	Death of close family member
53	Personal injury or illness
50	Marriage
47	Loss of job
45	Marital reconciliation
45	Retirement
44	Change in health of family member
40	Pregnancy
39	Sex difficulties
39	Gain of new family member
38	Change in financial status
37	Death of close friend
36	Change to different kind of work
35	Increase/decrease in arguments w/spouse
31	Taking out big mortgage on home
30	Foreclosure of mortgage or loan
30	Change in work responsibility
29	Child leaving home
28	Outstanding personal achievement
28	Spouse begins or stops work
24	Revision of personal habits

23   Trouble w/business superior
20   Change in work hours/condition
20   Change in residence
20   Change in school
19   Change in recreation
18   Change in social activities
16   Taking out small mortgage on home
16   Change in sleeping
15   Change in #s of family gatherings
15   Change in eating habits
13   Vacation
11   Minor violation of law

If your life-change values total 150–199, you stand a mild chance of suffering some illness in the next year.

200–299, posts a moderate risk.

Over 300 puts you in the group that is very likely to suffer serious physical or emotional illness.[2]

Job-related stress is probably one of the most common maladies in contemporary society. While the rating chart above covers nearly every aspect of life, it is rare to be able to measure the level of stress that our jobs create. Below is an exercise that has been helpful to many people.

What's Your Job-Stress Index?

Answer "Yes" or "No" to whether or not these common indicators of job stress apply to you. Then tally your answers to see how stressful your job really is.

1. Do you have little or no control over your job, how it's defined, and/ or how you're supposed to perform it?
2. Are you often overworked (e.g., could you do a better job if you had more time)?
3. Is it harder to make decisions at work?
4. Has the quality of your work deteriorated (e.g., do you make excuses or tell lies to cover up poor work)?
5. Are you unable to keep up with new equipment or methods that your job requires?
6. Has your company recently reorganized, merged with, or been taken over by another company, which you feel threatens your job?
7. Do you feel that management and/or your co-workers are openly or

covertly biased against older workers?
8. Is it harder for you to go to work (e.g., do you often go to work late or take days off because you don't feel up to it)?
9. Do you find yourself losing your temper at work over things you know to be trivial?
10. Have you suddenly become accident-prone?
11. Are you drinking more during or after work?
12. Are you experiencing physical symptoms that occur only, or are more pronounced, at work (e.g., dizziness, headaches, nervous stomach, back pain, or heart palpitations)?

SCORING:

Three or more "Yes" answers: You are experiencing some degree of job stress.

Five or more "Yes" answers: You are experiencing enough job stress to threaten your career.[3]

Choices

In a fast-paced life requiring multiple roles and making incessant demands upon us, we can take steps to reduce stress. Amy is a high-speed woman in a petite body whose mind-bending migraines bring her to a screeching halt. Last autumn the headaches became so intense the doctor ran her through a series of tests for brain tumors. Finding nothing, he ordered: Change the way you live your life. So she gave up her committee work, her outlets for music, her extra involvements. Her children won't show her the volunteer forms from school; instead, they inventory the cabinets and sign up to bring something they already have. Notices to make cookies and requests for chaperons disappear in school wastebaskets. The family has teamed up to eliminate stressors from Amy's life, helping her symptoms.

Fortunately, Amy's busyness was not based on low self-esteem; eliminating the extracurricular involvement could have resulted in an emotional crash had she been active due to feelings of inferiority in God's sight. Sorting out *why* we engage in such drastic overload is crucial to handling the change in a healthy way. It's not how much we do, it's why we do the things we do. After looking at the reasons behind the activity, we can work on the stressors.

Still, we have to find ways to deal with the stressors we can't sidestep or eliminate.

Stress-Out!

Various ways exist for dealing with unavoidable stress. One friend, whose stress levels seem to level off at nine on a ten-point scale, runs every day. Joelle combats stress by blocking out time for a regular bubble bath and a book. Gardening relieves stress for Ann. A ten-minute nap on a heating pad is Chloe's favorite therapy. One woman, a chaplain supervisor, recommended that her intern take a mini-vacation every day: five minutes to relax the mind and retreat mentally to a favorite vacation spot. Laughter is a documented stress-reducer; one psychologist advised, "Laugh every day before breakfast!"

Something I noticed about myself and relationships is that if I don't handle a misunderstanding immediately, I create a backlog of problems. They grow like a sponge in a gelatin capsule plastered with the label "Warning! Do not take internally!" because it expands 300 percent when wet. I end up with huge misconstrued impressions, many of which I imagined and could have let go had I aired them right away. And this list expands like that sponge, filling my soul and squeezing out God and others until I'm bursting with the stress.

Dealing with relationship issues as they arise takes care of the cumulative weight and its accompanying stress. Sometimes I simply ask, "That sounded like you meant _____. Is that what you meant?" This opens the way for clarity. Ephesians 4:26–27 resonates both health and spiritual wisdom: "Do not let the sun go down on your anger, and do not give the devil an opportunity."

Stress-Guards

In addition, stress is exacerbated by misunderstanding our value in Christ, by lack of purpose, and by poor boundaries.

Looking at my life responses, I've noticed that stress finds a receptive target when my sense of worth is at low ebb. When feeling inadequate, I'm much more likely to boil over at the innumerable interruptions in daily life, or at a letter that appears to be attacking my capabilities in a certain area, or at a comment intended to be helpful but which veered so far left it pierced my heart. My response to stress becomes a spiritual issue: if my intimacy level with God is high, then my self-image is positive, and I can choose not to receive some of the stressors as a direct challenge to my self-worth.

With a strong life-purpose, we can instantly repel certain things because we know they have little or no impact on our lives. This technique is similar to the "Save the big guns for the big battles" strategy: running events through a life grid before deciding how much weight to attach to them and how much emotional and mental involvement to give. "Will this matter a year from now? Ten years from now?" If not, we can let it go.

A heart attack in his early forties and persistent high blood pressure warned my father-in-law to mend his ways. He eliminated what stressors he could. For the rest, he recites the Serenity Prayer: "God, grant me the serenity to accept the things I cannot change, the courage to change those I can, and the wisdom to know the difference." Sometimes, he says, "I'll pray that prayer fifty times a day." My friend Steve carries a card stating, "Do not emotionally resist that which you cannot physically change."

With proper boundaries, we can refuse to allow certain arrows over the walls and into our spirits. Once while driving on the interstate, a car merged too far, nearly causing me to wreck. When the driver made obscene gestures at me, I refused to waste emotional energy over something I could not change. Not granting the other driver power over me deflected an obvious stressor.

A Powerful Shield

All of these stress-guards have one thing in common: a reflective life. Reflection may be one of the most powerful shields of all in deflecting stress. Taking time to monitor our moments and our days, we are led into a quiet place. There we find God and pour out our souls to Him. This quiet place is a receptacle for stress-related anxiety.

Looking at the life of David, we see a man pursued at every turn, whether by his former friend and colleague King Saul, or by enemies of the crown. I can't imagine a more stressful life, yet at every turn David turned to God. His reaction to stress was to seek comfort, direction, and peace from the Lord. Here, safe under the wings of the Almighty, David's soul found restoration; here he found wisdom to deal with the stress agents (like King Saul with an arrow meant for David!); here he feasted at a banquet in the presence of his enemies. In the midst of constant attacks and bloody battles and family feuds, David's perspective originated in God: "Surely goodness and lovingkindness will follow me all the days of my life, and I will dwell in the house of the Lord forever" (Psalm 23:6).

Cradled in the arms of God, sheltered by the almighty wings, the frayed edges of our spirits mend; our souls are restored; our perspective is renewed. The greatest stress-reducer of all infuses us: the grace and peace of our Lord Jesus. May you retreat in your anguish to the Father, and find once again the One who will hold you in your tears, comfort you in your fears, and protect you from your enemies.

May God be your resting place.

Quotes for Contemplation

Most of my personal stress reduction comes from . . . this: choosing daily to undergird my life with spiritual support. . . . The God-related day makes a vast difference in soothing the hectic pace we often find ourselves getting into. As we put our trust in God, we are mentally putting ourselves into God's time frame instead of living in our own. In God's time frame, it is natural to take life as it comes. . . . The de-stressor is that God expects of us no more than what our capabilities, time, and opportunity allow.

—MARGARET HOUK,
LIGHTEN UP AND ENJOY LIFE
MORE: EVERYDAY WAYS TO DE-
STRESS YOUR LIFESTYLE

Stress can catapult us (body and soul and spirit) down a steep bank into the sea, like the pigs rushed to their doom when the demons entered them; or stress can propel us straight into God, deepening and strengthening our faith and our reliance on God in the midst of it.

—JANE A. RUBIETTA

Years ago, I went to Canada and spent some time with Dr. Hans Selye, the Austrian-born physician who was the world's greatest authority on stress. As we walked through his laboratories, I asked Dr. Selye about his experiments with animals.

"Well," said Dr. Selye, "one thing I've observed is that animals are free of one kind of stress that can be very damaging to people. Do you know what it is?"

I had to shake my head.

"It's the stress," said Dr. Selye, "that comes from trying to be something you're not. No animal is guilty of this, but you see it everywhere in our society. The woman of fifty who tries to look and act as if she were twenty-five. The insecure businessman who poses as a great expert in his field when actually his knowledge is quite limited. The individual who puts on a great show of piety when his private life is full of dishonesty. Jesus

likened such hypocrites, you remember, to whitewashed tombs, clean and shining on the outside, but full of rottenness within.

"People who try to be something they're not put themselves under stress. They're always afraid of having their bluff called, or their pretense uncovered, or their inadequacy revealed. Whether these fears are realized or not, the stress is there, day after day, year after year, and in the end it takes its toll.

"That's why I like to step back from time to time," the doctor said, "and look for traces of this foolishness in my own life. Then I try to get rid of them and be myself. That way I know I'll live longer."

—**ARTHUR GORDON,**
DAILY GUIDEPOSTS 1995

Learning to pay attention to the present, choosing to find joy in the current moment, keeps stress at bay by freeing us from worrying about the future. If we bank all our hopes on what we've planned, rather than the way a situation actually turns out, we are bound to be disappointed. Learning to flex in the face of the unexpected can save us a great deal of stress.

One of the most covert forms of stress is unresolved pain from the past. Say, for instance, I had a fear of authority figures as a child. Now, when in the presence of people in authority, this hidden fear produces stress in many of my relationships, and makes me afraid to take the initiative. So I choose to react to life, rather than act. Such a passive stance creates enormous resistance to what God would have me to do, and sets up an internal stress reaction. Regardless of the type of unresolved pain, it leads us into stress.

—**JANE A. RUBIETTA**

God, grant me the serenity to accept
the things I cannot change,
The courage to change the things I can,
And the wisdom to know the difference;
Living one day at a time, enjoying one moment at a time,
Enjoying hardship as a pathway to peace;
Taking as He did, the sinful world as it is,
Not as I would have it,
Trusting that He will make all things right
If I surrender to His will,
That I may be reasonably happy in this life

And supremely happy with Him forever in the next.
Amen

—REINHOLD NIEBAHR

Scriptures for Meditation

"Come to Me, all who are weary and heavy-laden, and I will give you rest. Take My yoke upon you, and learn from Me, for I am gentle and humble in heart; and you shall find rest for your souls. For My yoke is easy, and My load is light."

—MATTHEW 11:28–30

Be anxious for nothing, but in everything by prayer and supplication with thanksgiving let your requests be made known to God. And the peace of God, which surpasses all comprehension, shall guard your hearts and your minds in Christ Jesus.

—PHILIPPIANS 4:6–7

Whatever is true, whatever is honorable, whatever is right, whatever is pure, whatever is lovely, whatever is of good repute, if there is any excellence and if anything worthy of praise, let your mind dwell on these things.

—PHILIPPIANS 4:8

We shall not turn back from Thee;
Revive us, and we will call upon Thy name.
O Lord God of hosts, restore us;
Cause Thy face to shine upon us, and we will be saved.

—PSALM 80:18–19

"For this reason I say to you, do not be anxious for your life, as to what you shall eat, or what you shall drink; nor for your body, as to what you shall put on. Is not life more than food, and the body than clothing?

"Look at the birds of the air, that they do not sow, neither do they reap, nor gather into barns, and yet your heavenly Father feeds them. Are you not worth much more than they?

"And which of you by being anxious can add a single cubit to his life's span?

"And why are you anxious about clothing? Observe how the lilies of

*the field grow; they do not toil nor do they spin, yet I say to you that even
Solomon in all his glory did not clothe himself like one of these.*

*"But if God so arrays the grass of the field, which is alive today and
tomorrow is thrown into the furnace, will He not much more do so for
you, O men of little faith?*

*"Do not be anxious then, saying, 'What shall we eat?' or 'What shall
we drink?' or 'With what shall we clothe ourselves?' For all these things
the Gentiles eagerly seek; for your heavenly Father knows that you need
all these things.*

*"But seek first His kingdom and His righteousness; and all these things
shall be added to you.*

*"Therefore, do not be anxious for tomorrow; for tomorrow will care for
itself. Each day has enough trouble of its own."*
                                    —MATTHEW 6:25–34

Journaling

Take some moments to stroll through your soul as you think about
stress. Do certain seasons of your life come to mind, certain feelings, impressions? Upon what reactions and resources did you rely?

Prayers of Confession, Praise, Petition

Paul, undoubtedly one of the more highly stressed individuals in Scripture, found ways to deal with the external demands of life (shipwreck, starvation, punishment, and torture). Read 2 Corinthians 4:6–11 and meditate on Paul's secret stress reliever. Flow from there into prayers of
confession, praise, and petition.

Moments for Creation

As you walk today, look around you. Stress appears nonexistent in the
created order. The birds go gladly about their life's work, the trees continue gently to grow and give leafy shelter, the brook flows without effort.
Let the peace of God seep from nature into your soul as you give over the
reins of control into your Savior's hands.

Silence

Reread the Scriptures in the meditation section. Is there a word or
phrase that stands out to you? Allow the Word of God to lead you into
silent contemplation on the protective, sheltering aspects of God.

Questions for Reflection ————————————

1. Notice physical, mental, and emotional reactions to stress. What happened before the stress reaction? Look beneath the event to understand your feelings about that event. (Example: Carla exploded at her children. Rather than simply manage her anger, she looked deeper to learn how she'd gotten to be so vulnerable to anger in the first place.)

2. For each of the following categories, write down the stresses that you currently feel:

   Financial:

   Relational:

   Vocational:

   Life change:

   Physical:

   Spiritual:

3. List some of the furor in your life right now. What elevates your stress level? When do you dip into adrenaline reserves? Do you long for a place of quiet rest? Jot down some ideas for creating quiet places, times in God's presence when you can reduce the stress.

4. Keep a journal of your stressors this week and how you handled them. Keep track, too, of any physiological reactions to the stress. Aches, pains, insomnia, pounding heart, anger, etc. Do you find certain times of the day or specific days are more stressful than others?

5. If symptoms of stress beg for your attention, it is time to reevaluate

your priorities. What circumstances can you change? How much of your stress is related to your inability to control life? What boundaries can you erect to keep from internalizing those unchangeables as stress? The object is not the absence of stress but the peace and presence of Christ in the midst of it.

Hymn of Praise ————————————————————

NEAR TO THE HEART OF GOD

There is a place of quiet rest,
Near to the heart of God;
A place where sin cannot molest,
Near to the heart of God.

O Jesus, blest Redeemer,
Sent from the heart of God,
Hold us who wait before Thee
Near to the heart of God.

There is a place of comfort sweet,
Near to the heart of God;
A place where we our Savior meet,
Near to the heart of God.

O Jesus, blest Redeemer,
Sent from the heart of God,
Hold us who wait before Thee
Near to the heart of God.

There is a place of full release,
Near to the heart of God;
A place where all is joy and peace,
Near to the heart of God.

O Jesus, blest Redeemer,
Sent from the heart of God,
Hold us who wait before Thee
Near to the heart of God.

—CLELAND B. MCAFEE

CHAPTER EIGHT

Friendships: Sentries of the Soul

We are circus performers without a protective net, women trapped in superficial relationships, alone in a crowd. What do we need to become the women God intended? Friendships play a crucial role in directing our lives.

The ocean roared a background accompaniment to the splashing of toddlers in the baby pool. A friend and I lazed in deck chairs, watching our children explore the sun-warmed water.

"Shut the gate, please!" I called to a woman who followed her child into the small pool. "Lift one end and slip the lever over."

Before she could respond, a three-year-old raced through the opening, intent on a visit to the "big people's" pool. The heavy gate shut with difficulty, and others invariably left it open, exposing children to the risk of drowning in the pool or the ocean.

"I feel like a gatekeeper," I said to Sheryl, after the fourteenth trip to shut the gate.

Sheryl squinted through sunglasses. "Why do you get up?"

"To keep our kids and the other children safe."

"Let the other people take care of their own kids, Jane."

Her bluntness silenced me. Later, walking along the beach, cold surf nibbled my ankles like a Chihuahua that misunderstood the command "Heel!" I wondered about her statement. Don't we need people who will stand watch at the gate? Where are the sentries who guard the thresholds of our souls? Who will speak the truth in love? Who questions our balance, priorities, and goals?

In the Old Testament, gatekeepers had a simple job: to keep watch at the gates of the temple and of the city. If a marauding band of renegades stormed across the land, guards blew a ram's horn, or shofar, to alert the people. If merchants sold goods on the Sabbath, gatekeepers sent them packing, thus guarding Israel's integrity. The Lord instituted the Sabbath "blue law," forbidding work on the holy day, not because all work and no play makes Jack a dull boy, but because focusing on *our* responsibility we forget that *He* is the One in whom we live, and move, and have our being.

Perhaps the problem lies in our definition of *friend*. Even Webster, who first defines friend as "one attached to another by affection or esteem," next calls a friend "an acquaintance."

We have scads of casual acquaintances: at work, in the neighborhood, at church. We live on the surface of relationships like waterbugs, never going below the water, much less into the deep. When Lillian Rubin conducted research, she asked the interviewees whom they would list as close friends. Contacting those people, Dr. Rubin asked them the same question. Too frequently, the second round of people contacted did not even mention the initial interviewee as a close friend.[1]

In a society where loneliness has clawed its way to prominence as a top women's issue, perhaps that's no surprise. True friends seem like a nearly nonexistent priority. Friendships rank at the bottom of the list for many busy women, crowded out by people whose needs and wants cry louder and longer, like squalling, brawling siblings demanding a seat at the right hand.

Many women, content to be surviving the daily footrace, seem unaware that races are run more easily with companions. The lack of intimacy in relationships is in complete denial of the way we are made. When God created Adam in the Garden, everything was "very good" except, He said, "It is not good . . . to be alone" (Gen. 2:18). We were designed for relationships; it is one of our primary longings as human beings, made in God's image.

Unfortunately, with a high premium on privacy, this longing constantly wars with an innate tendency toward self-preservation and safety. Intimacy, God's idea, is the opposite of isolation. Isolation is the enemy's strategy.

In contemplating the isolated path many of us tread, I've wondered if we need to redefine friend. Consider this: "*Friend:* n. [gatekeeper] one who will speak the truth in love out of concern for another's life before God; someone who will risk his/her relationship with a person in order to help that person."[2]

For many, however, the risk-taking relationship is rare.

One-Way Friendships

Kathryn and I have known each other for nearly a decade, though now we maintain our relationship long-distance. When her home went on the market, the realtor recommended intensive yard work to spruce up the landscaping. I took a day and drove the thirty minutes to her home, bringing gardening tools and gloves. While we worked side by side in 100-degree heat, sweat pouring off our brows and soaking our clothes, her cordless phone rang.

"Hi, Kathryn! We heard you're moving! Want to come out for lunch with Julie and me?"

"Oh, listen, thanks, but Jane is here and we're doing yard work to get the house ready to sell. . . ."

The silence on the other end spoke volumes. Eventually the caller hung up. Lunch dates were nice, but yard work . . . well.

Ironically, these very friends did not hesitate to call Kathryn in a pinch. Child care, a casserole, emergency counsel: if they needed assistance, they knew whom to ask, because when Kathryn heard of a need, she asked a gentle question: "How can I help?" But in the face of Kathryn's tangible needs, her friends vanished.

Party friends are lovely, but this sort of lopsided, one-way helping relationship is not on my list of definitions for intimacy. Many conscientious women give generously of themselves to others. While this may be the safest type of relationship, can we call it friendship? Genuine friendship implies mutuality and cannot exist without trust. And trust brings no guarantees.

The Trust Factor

We live in a world of safety chains, dead bolts, and neighborhood watches. We lock our computers, our doors, and our briefcases. Jostle a car and a siren blares that can be heard in the next block. Open a window and the security people are on the phone or the police are at the door. Politicians cut back-room deals, and the neighbor stabs us in the back. When our children turn two, we teach them about stranger danger and bad touch. Crime is up, murder is up, unemployment is up, and people are frustrated.

This is not Mayberry. We carry Mace and get a black belt in martial arts for protection. We can't leave keys in the car or windows open at night. And as we lock up for the evening, we lock our souls into tight, polite smiles. All the while, the longing for intimacy, for trusting relationships, gnaws holes in our stomach lining and eats away at our marriages.

Harriet Goldhor Lerner defines an intimate relationship as "one in which neither party silences, sacrifices, or betrays the self and each party expresses strength and vulnerability, weakness and competence in a balanced way."[3] In friendship, we can be ourselves and allow the other person to do the same.

Maybe we can't trust others and move toward genuine intimacy because we don't know ourselves. Who am I, really, when not molded by another's expectations? What do I love? What do I hate? What makes me angry? What do I fear? What are my pet peeves? What do I want out of life? What makes me laugh? The better we know ourselves, the better we can be known.

In order for a real relationship to exist, in order for us to be known, we must give up safety and control. We must wage war with the whisper "Don't trust," for we listen to our peril.

To be in relationship is to risk. To risk being known and knowing. To risk listening, to risk reevaluating our own beliefs, to risk change. Refusing to risk intimacy bears a high price.

Why Friends?

I scanned the crowded restaurant, looking for familiar faces. Finally someone turned and waved me over; hugs and coos and *how are you*'s ensued. I stashed my bulging red bag under the chair.

"Are you going to order French fries, Jane, extra crispy?" Pat asked. "I meant to bring you M&Ms to go with your coffee." These women knew my quirks and qualms, and they remembered.

We laughed, and I surveyed my longtime friends. Hair and weight had changed, but these women remained staunch warriors: in prayer and in relationship. How often had we cried, laughed, and prayed together? Because I was moving again, this time farther away than thirty minutes, we'd staged our first reunion in four years. Someone suggested we take turns filling in the gaps. They looked at me, the only semi-distant friend.

Tears came to my eyes as I pulled the stuffed manila envelopes from my bag and laid them on the table.

"My dream started here, in this circle. You first encouraged me to write, to pursue that dream." Resting my hands on the envelopes, I continued. "Here are originals of the nearly fifty articles I've had published since I moved. I wanted to show you, because you've had a huge hand in shaping my future. Thank you."

These friends had become a mirror for me, highlighting my gifts, understanding my weaknesses, helping me to get to know myself, and urging me forward.

A good friend also energizes us, feeding us creatively. For years Patti and I met weekly at 6:00 A.M. for coffee, bareing parts of our souls hidden to the rest of the world. And every week as we hugged good-bye and went on our ways, I left with new thoughts, questions I might not have asked. Many tears shed there found places for healing; many articles began around those coffee cups. Creativity glowed from Patti, and I caught it, without fail. She pushed me toward new frontiers in my thinking and my faith.

Like the gatekeepers of old, friends also sound the shofar when danger approaches, when we lean the wrong way, when we're tempted to take a wrong step. Once when my income was sporadic and Rich's salary didn't cover our expenses, I investigated the possibility of substitute teaching.

"Forget it, Jane," said Lynn, a former teacher. "You can't afford to get a job just to pay the bills. Who you are becoming is at stake, too, and I want to see you fulfill your goals. Teaching has never been a desire of yours. Besides, you need your emotional energy for your family. We'll pray for ways to make ends meet that are in line with your interests."

As a gatekeeper, knowing me well enough to know when I was about to make a mistake, Lynn held me accountable for both my gifts and my family responsibilities.

Another benefit to friendships is seen in our homes. As a newlywed, I became so wrapped up in my husband and our new life together that I began to overload our union with my needs. It isn't realistic or even fair to expect a spouse or one friend to meet all those needs. Friends broaden our support base and breathe new life into our homes.

Life-Giving

Support relationships are not a luxury. One study found that "people with many social ties (marriage, close friendships, extended families, church membership, or group associations) had a far lower mortality rate than those who lacked quality or depth in their social support systems." Another "indicated that men in their fifties, at high risk because of a low social and economic status, but who score high on an index of social networks, lived far longer than high status men with low social network scores."[4]

Gatekeepers—real friends—can literally save our lives. They can also keep us healthy. "James J. Lynch, a leading specialist in psychosomatic medicine at the University of Maryland, argues that social isolation brings emotional and then *physical deterioration*. Disease, he suggests, can be 'loneliness induced.' Lynch stresses the importance of the family and of caring relationships for friends and neighbors. 'Simply put there is a biological basis for our need to form human relationships. If we fail to fulfill that need, our health is in peril.' "[5]

With all these benefits, good friends make sense.

Stand Watch at the Portals

"Keep your eyes peeled," my brother ordered from inside the clubhouse. While the term taken literally is dubious, I knew my job: be on the lookout from the tree-house post.

Even now, I post a lookout and "keep my eyes peeled": for people a step farther along the road than I am, for people who exhibit qualities I desire to emulate, for women who laugh easily, who think deeply. I watch for godly women with emotional maturity, who reflect on their lives and choose growth rather than stasis.

Because I need to know, and I need to be known, however difficult that process may be.

Reaching Toward Growth

Taking an active role in seeking women who would thus encourage us may not be second nature. During a time of sweeping loss and change, a time of emotional and spiritual barrenness, I became aware of the lack of women who stood at the portals. I knew I needed to make an important telephone call.

Silent and threatening, the phone glared from my desk. Beads of sweat decorated my brow. My pulse accelerated. Hearing children's feet thumping on the stairs outside my office, I turned toward the door with a weak smile. A diversion is nice in a tense setting. Rich appeared, kids at his side.

"Call her." Warm brown eyes softened the command, but it was, nonetheless, a command.

"I know. I will. I've memorized the number by now; I just have to pump up the courage to punch it in and stay on the line."

"You can do it, hon. She'll be glad you called." With that, my husband gathered assorted offspring and hustled them out the door. His voice trailed behind him. "Let's have an adventure while Mommy has some space."

The door slammed, leaving me again staring at the telephone.

Call her? How could I call this woman I'd never met? Her books had been watchmen at the gate, her talks were sentries guiding me to safety.

"Think, think, think," I urged myself, like Winnie-the-Pooh doing his hardest work. "Why do you *need* to call Elaine?"

Because there was no one in my life who could come alongside me. Because I seemed to continually be in the awkward position of having no peers in ministry, of having no one willing to take me under her wings and teach me to fly more efficiently. Because I frequently felt like an alien, living in a land of strangers, and the landscape of my inner world seemed so different from others. Because, as I leaned on the portals of the door to my soul, I looked. And saw no one guarding the gate for me.

In the end I called Elaine, asking with quavering voice if she would consider mentoring me. This wise woman asked hard questions; questions that needed answers before we could further explore a mentoring relationship. Graciously, Elaine agreed to meet with me in several months, when she would be speaking in my area. And I agreed to do some homework.

Ironically, that phone call and its resultant homework put me in touch with seminaries and denominational leaders across the country, and literally changed the course of my life. One call spawned speaking engagements and writing projects; contacts with people who might function as spiritual soul-models; and a burden for women who day after day go through life without support.

For two years, seven of us have met at Elaine's as a covenant group. Much of the time I am quiet; as the youngest member, I have grown as a result of being free to observe and partake of their transparency, maturity, and loving acceptance. This circle calls me to accountability, growth, and depth in my relationships.

Able to Stand Guard

Much water has washed over the sands of my life since I first began seeking these sentries for the soul.

"I need to be the kind of friend I want to have," I said once to my husband in the midst of my aloneness and loneliness. Knowing this, even as we scan the horizon for gatekeepers, may we grow more deeply into women able to stand guard for one another.

Quotes for Contemplation ————————————————

Our well-developed ideology about marriage and the family, our insistence that these are the relationships that count for the long haul, have, I believe, blinded us to the meaning and importance of friendship in our lives. Until the soaring divorce rate pointed so sharply to a crisis in marriage, we still expected that all our needs for emotional intimacy, social connectedness and intellectual stimulation would be met there. Today we know better. But the knowledge of this reality, no matter how powerfully it has made itself felt, has failed to correct the fantasy.

—**LILLIAN B. RUBIN,**
JUST FRIENDS: THE ROLE OF
FRIENDSHIP IN OUR LIVES

A man can keep his sanity and stay alive as long as there is at least one person who is waiting for him. The mind of man can indeed rule his body even when there is little health left. A dying mother can stay alive to see her son before she gives up the struggle, a soldier can prevent his mental and physical disintegration when he knows that his wife and children are waiting for him. But when "nothing and nobody" is waiting, there is no chance to survive in the struggle for life.

—**HENRI NOUWEN,**
THE WOUNDED HEALER

Psychiatry must be concerned with two basic psychological needs: (1) the need to love and be loved and, (2) the need to feel that we are worthwhile to ourselves and others.

—**WILLIAM GLASSER,**
REALITY THERAPY:
A NEW APPROACH TO PSYCHIATRY

We must love one another or die.

—**W. H. AUDEN, POET**

*Like a parasitic worm, loneliness feeds on the spirit—and kills it. It is an
existential misery. When the question "Why?" has no answer, neither does
the question "who?" Who am I? If all that I do is meaningless, so am I.
Personal meaning and human value arise only in relationship. Solitude
casts doubt on them. Identity, too, is discovered only in relationship.
Lacking companions at the level of the soul, I finally cannot find my soul.
It always takes another person to show myself to me. Alone, I die.*

—WALT WANGERIN,
AS FOR ME AND MY HOUSE

*Friendships can no more tolerate this sort of "unknowability" than
one's relationship to God, to a spouse, or to self can. Of course there are
friendships of varying levels and intensities, and the amount of
transparency will always differ. But one thing is certain in all of these
relationships: the amount of transparency must be reasonably mutual on
both sides, or the friendship suffers. . . . In a relationship where there is
transparency there can be enormous growth. For as the windows become
unshaded, we permit others to offer light to our opinions, our concerns,
and our dreams. They help complete our thoughts, balance our extremes,
and correct our miscalculations. We are reminded of parallel situations
that we may have forgotten and that now bring encouragement, direction,
or prevention. They may have shared with us the very keys of life, which
may escalate our maturity or protect us from destruction. But
transparency has to happen first.*

—GORDON AND GAIL MACDONALD,
IF THOSE WHO REACH COULD
TOUCH

*Whether child or adult, it is friends who provide a reference outside
the family against which to measure and judge ourselves; who help us
during passages that require our separation and individuation; who
support us as we adapt to new roles and new rules; who heal the hurts
and make good the deficits of other relationships in our lives; who offer
the place and encouragement for the development of parts of self that, for
whatever reasons, are inaccessible in the family context. It's with friends
that we test our sense of self-in-the-world, that our often inchoate,
intuitive, unarticulated vision of the possibilities of a self-yet-to-become
finds expression.*

—LILLIAN B. RUBIN,
JUST FRIENDS: THE ROLE OF
FRIENDSHIP IN OUR LIVES

In a way—nobody sees a flower—really—it is so small—we haven't time—and to see takes time, like to have a friend takes time.

—GEORGIA O'KEEFE, PAINTER

The chief danger with friendships is expecting too much of them: expecting that in a friend we will find total, infinite love and acceptance such as only God can give; or expecting a friend to need us to give her life the meaning and depth that can only come from the love of God.

We cannot expect a friend to validate our worth, to make us feel important and needed. If we only truly know ourselves in relationship, then the ultimate relationship for self-knowledge and true acceptance is Jesus Christ. With Christ's love informing our beings, then all our relationships on earth mirror some facet of that love.

—JANE A. RUBIETTA

We are such an instant, self-absorbed, me-oriented society, where the whole idea of giving yourself to one another feels old-fashioned and foreign. We've moved into this idolatry of self where we're more concerned with what we get out of a friendship than with what we can give. We become our own idols in this life rather than icons in whom others can see God. Such superficial friendships are like instant mashed potatoes— not as satisfying as the real thing. But authentic friendship reaches out and gives rather than always taking. . . . It's Satan's satisfaction to split a friendship and keep two friends from reconciling. He wants to cause feuds and fragmentation. But friendship redeems. It pulls broken parts together and offers healing.

—LUCI SHAW,
VIRTUE

You have to move gradually from crying outward—crying out for people who you can think can fulfill your needs—to crying inward to the place where you can let yourself be held and carried by God, who has become incarnate in the humanity of those who love you in community. No one person can fulfill all your needs. But the community can truly hold you. The community can let you experience the fact that, beyond your anguish, there are human hands that hold you and show you God's faithful love.

—HENRI NOUWEN,
THE INNER VOICE OF LOVE

Scriptures for Meditation ─────────────────

Two are better than one because they have a good return for their labor. For if either of them falls, the one will lift up his companion. But woe to the one who falls when there is not another to lift him up.
—ECCLESIASTES 4:9–10

"This is My commandment, that you love one another, just as I have loved you. Greater love has no one than this, that one lay down his life for his friends. You are My friends, if you do what I command you."
—JOHN 15:12–14

"Blessed is the [one] who listens to me,
Watching daily at my gates,
Waiting at my doorposts."
—PROVERBS 8:34

"Son of man, I have appointed you a watchman to the house of Israel; whenever you hear a word from My mouth, warn them from Me."
—EZEKIEL 3:17

"Be on guard for yourselves and for all the flock, among which the Holy Spirit has made you overseers, to shepherd the church of God which He purchased with His own blood."
—ACTS 20:28

And [Jesus] took with Him Peter and the two sons of Zebedee, and began to be grieved and distressed. Then He said to them, "My soul is deeply grieved, to the point of death; remain here and keep watch with Me."

And He went a little beyond them, and fell on His face and prayed, saying, "My Father, if it is possible, let this cup pass from Me; yet not as I will, but as Thou wilt."

And He came to the disciples and found them sleeping, and said to Peter, "So, you men could not keep watch with Me for one hour? Keep watching and praying, that you may not enter into temptation; the spirit is willing, but the flesh is weak."
—MATTHEW 26:37–41

Faithful are the wounds of a friend. . . . Iron sharpens iron, so one

man sharpens another.
                              —PROVERBS 27:6, 17

*He who walks with wise men will be wise, but the companion of fools
will suffer harm.*
                              —PROVERBS 13:20

*That which we have seen and heard we declare to you, that you also
may have fellowship with us; and truly our fellowship is with the Father
and with His Son Jesus Christ.*
*But if we walk in the light as He is in the light, we have fellowship
with one another, and the blood of Jesus Christ His Son cleanses us from
all sin.*
                              —1 JOHN 1:3, 7, NKJV

Journaling

With blank paper before you, scribble some notes about your friendships, past and present, and your longings for friendship. Where is God
in the midst of your longings, and where do your current friends fit into
those longings? Perhaps instead of writing you will want to draw with cray-
ons or paint how you feel in relationships.

Prayers of Confession, Praise, Petition

Take some time to dig around in the basement of your heart. Invite the
Lord to examine the junk and make a clean sweep. With a clean heart it's
so easy to turn to a time of praise, and then in humility place problems
and petitions in the Lord's all-loving, all-capable hands.

Moments for Creation

Praise seems to come naturally from time spent in creation. Let everything you see become an icon, directing your thoughts and prayers to the
Creator. May you be refreshed spiritually, mentally, emotionally, physically, by the time outside, walking in the garden with God.

Silence

As you move into silence, ask yourself where you fall on the loneliness
versus intimacy scale. Invite the Lord to show himself to you in the quiet.
Let Him wrap you in His love during this silence.

Questions for Reflection ——————————————

1. Evaluate and list the different roles you carry. Now list the person/people who support and challenge you in each role. How often do you have significant interaction with each person? What would be ideal? Which roles are wholly or largely unsupported? What is God revealing about His desire for you?

2. List the people you would term "friends." Take an honest look at the give-and-take qualities of these relationships. Is there reciprocity? Perhaps you could make two columns: one for people who offer support to you, another for those who ask for support from you. Does a pattern emerge? If so, can you explore the underlying reasons?

3. What prevents you from establishing and maintaining healthy supportive contact with others? What issues hinder you? Is it the "I don't deserve it, I can't afford it" mentality? "Don't talk, don't trust, don't feel"?

4. In what ways do you fear intimacy? Fear of abandonment? Fear you won't be loved or accepted? Fear of betrayal? Fear that you can't be the friend? That you can't listen, learn, love? Fear that you'll be taken advantage of?

5. How is your trust factor? How much of yourself are you willing to share with another? What holds you back?

6. Have you a friendship that has been split apart by something in the past? While resuming that relationship may not be possible, forgiveness and/or reconciliation are. What is the Lord directing you to do?

Hymn of Praise

BLEST BE THE TIE THAT BINDS

Blest be the tie that binds
Our hearts in Christian love;
The fellowship of kindred minds
Is like to that above.

Before our Father's throne
We pour our ardent prayers;
Our fears, our hopes, our aims are one,
Our comforts and our cares.

We share each other's woes,
Our mutual burdens bear;
And often for each other flows
The sympathizing tear.

When we asunder part,
It gives us inward pain;
But we shall still be joined in heart,
And hope to meet again.

—JOHN FAWCETT

CHAPTER NINE

Restored by Beauty

*As women, we identify with our surroundings.
Our soul is nourished by beauty, yet too often
we deny ourselves this healing poultice.
Learning to incorporate beauty into our lives
without guilt will hasten our healing and
bring us to wholeness.*

Fall of 1995 was the hardest season of many for me. The mother role
pressed me into intense chauffeuring responsibilities. Because we lived
on the "other" side of town—the side where the piano lessons, park district, ice rink, band, and preschool weren't—I trekked the thirty-minute
round trip up to ten times each week. Three hundred minutes I shuttled
loved ones to lessons and classes and sports programs; this did not include
the events that took place on our side of town in which our children (and
thus, their mother) also participated.

The upshot of this brief history of insanity is this: total physical exhaustion and a hunger to experience the goodness of God battled within
like twins fighting in the womb. Stretched to the breaking point, my body
began exhibiting a wide variety of signs of poor health.

Not only my body, but my soul. I rediscovered a martyr tendency. I lost
weight; my face grew thin, my journal entries slim, my spiritual appetite
negligible.

Finally, a loving group of women held me in my tears, prayed for me, talked with me about this spiritual anorexia, this deprivation of soul resulting from constant output.

This was a soul-famine, unlike any I'd experienced. Outwardly, I exhibited also sorts of fruit speaking and writing. Inwardly, my dehydrated soul left me emaciated. I drew from a well gone dry. Job's words jarred me: "My gauntness rises up and testifies against me" (16:8, NIV).

One of these precious women shared her life goal: to find, and express to others, the beauty around her.

I'd tried to keep up prayer, Scripture, and journaling, but beauty . . . beauty was far from my spiritually shuttered eyes.

At the time, we lived in a near-urban neighborhood devoid of beauty. One of my first acts upon moving in was to rip out all the half-dead, weed-consumed shrubs in front of the house. Over time, a perennial garden became a place to find God.

But I failed to transfer that "beauty lesson" into the rest of my life. I became sensory-deprived, unable to perceive the glory of God in nature. My inability to do so nearly led to a breakdown. As my friends upheld me, they wondered aloud how far away a breakdown could be.

A Theology of Beauty

This new beauty regimen took some convincing. I examined my theology of leisure. Like a person who compulsively denies herself food, we may compulsively deny ourselves what our spirits need. Many of us still do the things directly related to, obviously akin to, soul-care: reading Scripture, praying, etc. But we starve ourselves of other life-giving elements.

Why? Because we don't *deserve* the nurture? Because no one else we know takes time out to find God in the beauty of this created earth? Because people might think we're selfish? We take time for haircuts, television, ice cream, and telephone calls; but intentional time spent alone in a place of beauty might be regarded as an egocentric pursuit.

One of the commandments tells us to deny ourselves and do no work. Part of the Sabbath is enjoying the work already done on our behalf: by God, and through His creation. But are we so busy striving—for what? equality? the status of a career? a "better" lifestyle? respect?—that we cannot take time to be still and know that God is God? Our tendency as humans is to indulge the lie that work is our salvation, our meaning, our power. When we fail to cease, to rest, when we forget to look at the One who created us, we are in danger of idolatry, of finding our sole (and soul) meaning in the works of our hands.

As women, roles, expectations, and reality crush us in their mortar and pestle. It's easy to ignore the gnawing hunger of our hearts for a beauty totally outside of our responsibilities.

I am learning that I cannot live, love, and work out of my emptiness; that I function best out of fullness; that I maximize the output by first refueling. That's what these personal retreat days are about. But in between, we need pit stops.

Beauty provides the pit stops so we can continue the race.

Beauty School 101

Beauty is an icon, pointing us to God. It is not God, is not to be worshiped, but is to lead us into worship of our Creator.

The beauty of the created world schools me. Beauty brings me closer to God. I discover more about the Creator as I spend time admiring His creation.

In my first beauty lesson, I met a God who delights in extravagance. As we drove through our neighborhood, Josh exclaimed, "Look, Mom! It's snowing!" White stuff blew thickly about, lining gutters, pooling up in clouds of fluff near buildings. But with the thermometer hovering at seventy degrees, this white came from cottonwood trees, sending countless seeds to replant the earth. If the cottonwood becomes extinct, it won't be God's fault!

I'm also recognizing, in my loneliness, that when I long to be surrounded by the arms of God, creation is one place to find Him. Beauty is a tangible link with our Creator, an assignation with the great Lover of our souls, the Artist of the universe. Beauty shifts our focus from intellectual Christianity into a sensory mode, where we perceive God through interacting with our surroundings. This external sanctuary draws us more deeply into a love relationship with Him. And the aching loneliness is filled.

This ode to beauty also demonstrates our honor of God: honoring His genius, His sheer delight in beauty; honoring His work on our behalf. In stopping the restless pacing of the soul, we demonstrate trust and faith. Trust that God will love us even when we aren't working; faith in God's infinite care for us, in His desire to fill us with all good things.

In a hopeless world, beauty is inextricably wrapped with hope, reaffirming God's presence, His creative love, His joyful extravagance. Beauty reminds us of the smallness of our worlds—giving us perspective on our limited control—and jogs our memories about Who is in charge. Beauty is a healing agent for souls worn by work, worried by relationships, wearied by running. One of my days and nights of craziness found me outside the park district office, waiting for a ballet class to finish. I couldn't remember how I'd driven the car to that spot. I parked and turned off the ignition; evening settled around me. Remnants of the sun lingered over the golf course, painting the oaks golden. The wind picked up, flattening leaves against fences. A flag snapped; the car rocked gently. Surrounded by this bracing evidence of God, I adjusted the seat and slept.

Awakening, my mood lifted when Ruthie bounced toward the car. God's presence rejuvenated, restored, and readied me for the next lap around the track.

Beauty reminds me that I can't parent, write, or speak from an empty well. Without first refilling my soul with long draughts of God, I draw rocks instead of water. Here I witness the intricate connection between spirituality, energy, creativity, and beauty: these elements feed into one another, creating a whole larger than the sum of the parts.

Where to Find God: Mini Beauty Breaks

Combing the used book shelf, my breath nearly stopped when I pulled the aged volume down. Turning to the cover page, the copyright date jumped out: 1889! More than 100 years earlier, someone in England held this book, learned about God within this binding. Imagine. My pulse quickened when I spotted the sign: Hardcover Books, $1.00.

Books

Books are a source of beauty easily overlooked. By holding the pearly-paged, century-old text in my hand, I hold history, treasure, and beauty.

In the movie *Shawshank Redemption*, the wrongly convicted Andy DuFresne found sanity in the knowledge stored within his supple mind. When the opportunity came, he eagerly took his job assignment in the library. Once there, he wrote letters weekly to the state, requesting books and funds.

Finally, an angry guard shoved him toward the office, where Andy stumbled over crates full of books. The letter said they trusted this would satisfy him, and they considered the matter closed: "Please stop sending us letters." Andy's face ignited into joy. "It only took six years. From now on, I'll write two letters a week instead of one."

Books kept him sane, and expanded the world of the inmates beyond cement blocks.

Music

Another easily overlooked area of beauty is music. A Christian radio station plays an hour of contemplative music every evening from six to seven; I love it when the trip to a meeting falls during that hour. A friend plays Beethoven while she cleans her house, filling her soul and energizing her work.

A healing example of music flowed from *The Shawshank Redemption*. When Andy opened those boxes, he found a crate full of classical music. As the guard left the room, he pulled Mozart's *The Marriage of Figaro* out and reverently placed it on the record player. As music filled the room, the camera moved to the guard, temporarily indisposed, who called out in alarm.

Andy looked at the record, looked at a key, and locked the guard in the bathroom. He then set the loudspeaker next to the record player and turned on the microphone. All activity stopped across the entire compound. Prisoner and guard alike halted in their work and their leisure, frozen in place.

Red, an inmate who narrated the film, said, "I have no idea what those two Italian ladies were singing about. Truth is, I don't want to know. Some things are best left unsaid. I like to think they were singing about something so beautiful it could not be expressed in words.

"I tell you, those voices soared, higher and farther than anybody in a gray place dares to dream of. It was like some beautiful bird flapped into our drab little cage and made those drab walls dissolve away. And for the briefest of moments every man at Shawshank felt free."

The warden slammed Andy into solitary for two weeks. Coming out, disheveled and pale, he stated, "Easiest time I ever did." His lunch companions snorted in disbelief: "No such thing."

"Ah, I had Mister Mozart to keep me company."

"Did they let you tote the record player in there?" someone asked.

Andy said, "It was in here," pointing to his head, "in here," pointing to his heart. "That's the beauty of music. They can't take that from you. . . . You need it so you don't forget. Forget that there are places in the world that aren't made out of stone, that there's something inside that they can't get to, that they can't touch, that's yours."

"What are you talking about?"

"Hope."

Museums

During the autumn of my spiritual anorexia, we were given tickets to see the Monet exhibit at the Art Institute in Chicago. Imagine my beauty-deprived soul, surrounded by the works of the great Impressionist Claude Monet, who said, "I want to paint as a bird sings." Standing in the center of the galleries, headphones clapped to my ears, oblivious to pressing crowds, I wept as the beauty filled the hunger pockets of my being.

The word *muse* means, in its ancient Greek form, "to wonder or marvel"; today, it has come to mean "to become absorbed in thought, especially: to turn something over in the mind meditatively and often inconclusively." Growing up, museums seemed reserved for the highly intellectual, the culturally elite, those with money and time to spare. I am learning that museums reveal the glory and beauty of God, the vital importance of marvel and wonder, the necessity of cultivating gifts and talents in responsible ways.

Personal Pampering

The sound of water tumbling into the bathtub filled the air; steam rose, and with it bubbles, thick and luxurious. When I was a gangling, late-to-develop teenager, my mother understood the importance of pampering. She fixed a platter of special goodies—pepperoni, cheese, olives, crackers—creating a personal spa for me. Submerged in bubbles, with a book in my hands and snacks within reach, some of the painful wounds of adolescence healed.

When I felt far from feminine, my mother helped to create a sense of beauty within me. Now as an adult, I am relearning what it means to revel in my femininity. For a time, I would only go to retreat houses with bathtubs, because the luxury of a bath restored the fraying edges of my soul.

Personal pampering needn't be selfish. It's a way of honoring the woman God created us to be. Whether it's a candle by the bed, potpourri on the desk, a special perfume, or silky undergarments, beauty's restoration is not complete until personalized. Other possibilities: a leisurely sniff along the perfume counter at your favorite department store; a makeover at a cosmetic store; fresh flowers for the dinner table or dressing table; a feminine, fanciful accent to your decorating. I keep perfume samples in drawers, scenting the contents and reminding me every time I open them of the femininity of scent.

In the world as we now know it, women are not encouraged to be feminine. Masculinity demands emulation in careers and ladder-climbing; and much of our duties are relegated to left-brain, factual, organizational living. The world may demand masculine traits at times, but we needn't sacrifice the feminine.

Nature

Natalie stopped by, nervous with the energy of coping with two careers and a busy family. Pam, relaxing on the deck, greeted her warmly, urging the neighbor to pull up a chair.

"It's good to see you, Nat—" Pam's voice broke off, her face transformed with wonder. A hummingbird hovered near Natalie's head, the first Pam had seen since hanging up the bird feeder. Wordlessly, she pointed at the bird, inviting Natalie to come with her into the moment.

But Natalie was too intent on pressing on to reach the goal. She stated her business and hurried home, too harried to greet the presence of God on a wooded deck.

Too often we lower the shades of the windows to our souls, thinking nature superfluous for one person, though perfect for a rambunctious family outing. Intimate time with the Savior spent in creation reaps rewards far outweighing the time invested.

We don't have to have a week-long solitary retreat in a cabin (though it would be nice). Last week, on a rare fall day when the house inside was cooler than the outside, I stepped into the brilliant sun, blades of grass nipping my bare feet. The grass was so warm, the sunshine so inviting, I lay on the ground. Praise bubbled from my lips as the trees spiraled above me, stretching toward blue sky. "A sun sandwich!" I proclaimed with a crazed grin to a friend later. I think she was embarrassed, but blanketed between sun and green, I had worshiped God.

True Worship

Whether we find God most clearly and relevantly in music, books, a bubble bath, or nature, God desires that we bring an offering of praise. It seems to be a small enough sacrifice to rest in His created order, allowing Him to wrap loving arms about us. Because space doesn't come naturally in our tightly jammed lives, we must create room for God to speak, to woo, to love with the determination of a suitor held too long at arm's length. Today, let God bring you roses.

Quotes for Contemplation ————————————————————

Better than a room with four walls, nature is alive and speaks
restorative words to us, silent words of growth and dormancy, stability and

weakness, flower and weed, health and decay, life and death, and patience in process.

Frequently when drained in spirit myself, I have spent a day outside, watching the birds, feeling the snow fall, listening to the Voice in the quiet, and dwelling on Scripture. Belonging to the life behind nature can't help but rekindle even the weariest of hearts.

If we are always in the city surrounded by buildings which are large but not alive, we'll feel dwarfed. We may marvel at what great engineering and architectural minds have done, but we can't draw life and strength from steel and mortar. We draw life from what is alive!

The biographer of Brother Lawrence once wrote of that holy man:

"In the winter seeing a tree stripped of its leaves, and considering that within a little time the leaves would be renewed and after that the flowers and fruit would appear, he received such a high view of the providence and power of God which has never since been effaced from his soul."

Recognizing that it is Christ himself who "holds all things together," I see that same power possible in me and therefore through me to others.

—**GAIL MACDONALD,**
HIGH CALL, HIGH PRIVILEGE

Evolution may explain design, pattern, and function, but it doesn't explain beauty.

—**LYNN N. AUSTIN, AUTHOR**

The beauty was put there to make the pain endurable. The two must be inseparable. That is life: beauty, pain, love, and grace. It is enough. . . .

Seeking beauty, looking for it, raising our heads and eyes to it, putting ourselves in places of beauty: this is a creative response to pain. This is healing in itself.

I am thankful for choice. In fact, I'll make a choice right now: to live, to live, to live! Today I shall go to the monastery and accept the love of God. I shall sit in the sunshine. I shall drink the beauty of the trees, leaves, lake, mountains, birds, chapel—all of it. It is God's arm extended to me. I am not alone. Everywhere God surrounds me.

—**ELSIE NEUFELD,**
DANCING IN THE DARK

Vanity it is, to wish to live long, and to be careless to live well.

—**THOMAS À KEMPIS,**
THE IMITATION OF CHRIST

If a man finds himself with bread in both hands, he should exchange one loaf for some flowers of the narcissus, because the loaf feeds the body, but the flowers feed the soul.

—MOHAMMED (CA. A.D. 600)

The water laughs its way over a dam, shushing and giggling like children in church. The bridge spanning the narrow, rutted logging road invites me to sit and swing my legs, and I do, keeping time with the birds' joy song. This sanctuary for my soul fills me, feeds me; all around me I hear the voice of God.

—JANE A. RUBIETTA

Make room for that which is capable of rejoicing, enlarging, or calming the heart. . . .

—GERHARDT TERSTEEGEN (1649–1700)

Music takes us out of the actual and whispers to us dim secrets that startle our wonder as to who we are, and for what, whence, and whereto.

—RALPH WALDO EMERSON

I wondered over again for the hundredth time what could be the principle which, in the wildest, most lawless, fantastically chaotic, apparently capricious work of nature, always kept it beautiful. The beauty of holiness must be at the heart of it somehow, I thought. Because our God is so free from stain, so loving, so unselfish, so good, so altogether what He wants us to be, so holy, therefore all His works declare Him in beauty; His fingers can touch nothing but to mould it into loveliness.

—GEORGE MACDONALD

Scripture for Meditation

Finally . . . whatever is true, whatever is honorable, whatever is right, whatever is pure, whatever is lovely, whatever is of good repute, if there is any excellence and if anything worthy of praise, let your mind dwell on these things.

—PHILIPPIANS 4:8

The Lord is my shepherd, I shall not want.
He makes me lie down in green pastures;
He leads me beside quiet waters.
He restores my soul;
He guides me in the paths of righteousness
For His name's sake.
Even though I walk through
the valley of the shadow of death,
I fear no evil; for Thou art with me;
Thy rod and Thy staff, they comfort me.
Thou dost prepare a table before me
in the presence of my enemies;
Thou hast anointed my head with oil;
My cup overflows.
Surely goodness and lovingkindness will follow me
all the days of my life,
And I will dwell in the house of the Lord forever.

—PSALM 23

Let the mountains bring peace to the people,
And the hills, in righteousness.

—PSALM 72:3

"Therefore, I am now going to allure her;
I will lead her into the desert and speak tenderly to her.
There I will give her back her vineyards,
and will make the Valley of Achor a door of hope.
There she will sing as in the days of her youth,
as in the day she came up out of Egypt.
"In that day," declares the Lord, "you will call me 'my husband';
you will no longer call me 'my master.' "

—HOSEA 2:14–16, NIV

Journaling

Journal whatever thoughts come to mind about beauty: how you think about beauty, the place you've accorded it in your life, what God's purpose and response to beauty might be.

Prayers of Confession, Praise, Petition

Are there places in your own life where you have failed to create an atmosphere of beauty, whether your heart, your words, your relationships, your home? Spend time in confession now, considering these thoughts.

Praise comes naturally after meditating on the beauty around us. This is a great time to get outside man-made walls and let beauty soak into your soul, then permeate your praise.

Petition the Creator of order and beauty for the needs of those you love, including yourself. He delights to give gifts to His children.

Moments for Creation

Crunch through leaves, stroll among budding trees, rest on warm green grass, make a snow angel. Whatever season, whatever location, spend time extolling the Lord for all He has done on your behalf! I wish I could be with you, praising God together for His greatness.

Silence

Would you like to spend time in silence outside? Bring a journal and pen, and maybe a blanket, and wait on the Lord. What flowers will He bring today? Notes written after contemplative time in prayer will remind you tomorrow of His great love for you.

Questions for Reflection

1. What place most moves you with its beauty? What hinders you from getting there? When your spirit rises up in protest, list the excuses and reasons. Some are legitimate: child care, single parenting, uninvolved/ unavailable husband. What can you do to create space for yourself? (Suggestions: trade a morning each month with another mom, or a Saturday switch).

2. Where do you find—feel closest to—God? How often do you go there? What is God directing you to do?

3. Where does your theology fall on the lines of beauty, of treating your-

self to God's creation, and thus to the tangible presence of God? Is there a childhood tape playing, warning you of the dangers of being spoiled? Is taking time for beauty an illicit form of indulgence?

4. Check out the movie *Enchanted April*. Watch for themes of healing, renewal, restoration. What effects did this movie have on your perspective of relationships? Relaxation? Healing through beauty?

Hymn of Praise

JOYFUL, JOYFUL, WE ADORE THEE

Joyful, joyful, we adore Thee,
God of glory, Lord of love;
Hearts unfold like flowers before Thee,
Opening to the sun above.
Melt the clouds of sin and sadness;
Drive the dark of doubt away.
Giver of immortal gladness,
Fill us with the light of day!

All Thy works with joy surround Thee,
Earth and heaven reflect Thy rays,
Stars and angels sings around Thee,
Center of unbroken praise.
Field and forest, vale and mountain,
Flowery meadow, flashing sea,
Chanting bird and flowing fountain,
Call us to rejoice in Thee.

Thou art giving and forgiving,
Ever blessing, ever blest,
Well-spring of the joy of living,
Ocean depth of happy rest!
Thou our Father, Christ our brother,
All who live in love are Thine;

Teach us how to love each other,
Lift us to the joy divine.

Mortals, join the mighty chorus
Which the morning stars began;
Love divine is reigning o'er us,
Binding all within its span.
Ever singing, march we onward,
Victors in the midst of strive;
Joyful music leads us sunward,
In the triumph song of life.

—HENRY VAN DYKE

CHAPTER TEN

Nurturing Your Dream

*What dreams would God plant in the soil of
our souls, if only we would listen?
Is dreaming a privilege of a lost generation?
Or is it a device which can direct us
more deeply into the abundant life?*

Early-morning sun sliced through the mist. Rich and I sat at a restaurant,
coffee steaming before us. His inner ear is finely tuned, both as a musician
and as a counselor; he is deeply sensitive to chords of longing in others.
He heard a melody begin to form in my soul, and with the gentle hands
of an artist began to ease the song from its dark, locked box.

The song surprised me. Somewhere along the road of setting boundaries; of developing a God-honoring self-esteem; of plowing through
muddy fields of forgiveness; and of zooming through stress on adrenaline,
a deep and persistent longing began to hum within my tone-deaf soul. I
tuned in more frequently. What was this song to be? The longing sounded
like a desire to tell about the road of healing I'd traveled. At every turn I
found women in similar straits but with no vehicle to transport them down
the road.

Fear squeezed my vocal chords. I was afraid to sing this song aloud.
But the musician's sensitive hands coaxed music from a rusty instrument.

"I . . . I want to write," I whispered in that restaurant years ago. I swal-
lowed hard, trying to make room for the notes to come out, waiting for

courage to let them sing. "I want to speak. To share with other women what the Lord has done. I don't want them to struggle as long as I did; I don't want my sisters to labor in their loneliness."

The song has been long in coming, and with the song have come more tears. It is still in the writing and testing stages of composing. I remain a novice, sight-reading with my right hand, struggling to combine both hands, to master all the parts. But always, hovering over the lines of my life, a descant dance, reminding me of my dream, informing my days and my priorities. As a wife and a mother, I listen for the song, knowing that if I pay attention, others may one day hear music and begin to compose their own melodies.

I am not always a good student. Sometimes I am an errant child in a stifling band room in late spring, staring out the window, running in my imagination through a field a hundred miles away. The director calls me back to attention, tapping his baton on the music stand, that I might hear the soul-instruction.

Sometimes I compare my music, my inept fingerings, my inability to find the right pitch, with my neighbor's song and put down the instrument. But always I am called to pick it back up and to play my own song. For if I do not play, who will dance? Who will sing?

If the Holy Spirit is coaxing a new song from you, then open your mouth! In denying the dream we deny the work the Holy Spirit would do with it in others' lives. If we do not dream the melody, the ears that wait will not hear the music that will set them free. For our song is never intended for our ears alone, but to give grace and music and a new song to all who hear.

Longing to Dream

"There must be something more . . ." we sigh. "Something bigger than my laundry pile, more meaningful than the stacks of paper work on my desk." Whether the longing strikes when you're crunching numbers, or commuting, or listening to lyric opera, or changing a diaper, hidden within each of us is a desire for deeper and broader fulfillment, for a wider application of our lives than our day-to-day, pay-the-bills-feed-the-cat existence. A longing for something that goes beyond our daily routine.

This longing is contrary to the way many Christians exist. We may not hear about "longing" from the pulpit. In the asceticism of Christianity we may have decided that dreaming is *verboten*, that approving the things that are excellent automatically excludes luxuries like dreaming. Perhaps someone told us that dreaming was the opposite of self-denial; that Christians don't have time to dream. Our responsibilities suffocate our dreams.

We are busy people, masking our lack of purpose by our hectic pace. Masquerading as purposeful activity, busyness binds and gags our dreams. Like a kidnap victim, if we toss our dreams on the backseat long enough, a curious symptom emerges.

One of the tip-offs to hidden longing, to the dream I'd cast behind me, was, surprisingly, anger. I was angry at things I didn't like to do, at people who made incessant demands upon me, at this lagging in my spirit. I was angry when I left my house clean and returned that evening to a bomb site. Angry that I spent much of my life doing the urgent and the immediate but not necessarily the important.

I believe that dreaming is therapeutic, and that these longings are seeded in our souls by God. That if we listen closely, we'll hear a new song humming just below the noise of our lives. For years I kept Emmet Fox's words beside me as a reminder that listening to the dream was vital:

> But how is one to find [one's] true place in life? Is there any means whereby you may discover what it really is that God wishes you to do? You may feel inclined to say: "Even if it be true that God has some splendid thing that he wishes me to do, and to be, how can I possibly find out what it is?" Perhaps you may even be tempted to add: "I am a very plain, everyday sort of person; my circumstances are extremely restricted; the conditions of my life are just drab commonplace. How then can there be something wonderful, beautiful, splendid awaiting me? Or, even if there were, how could I possibly get to know about it?" And the answer is Divinely simple—already in your past life from time to time, God himself has whispered into your heart just that very wonderful thing, whatever it is, that he is wishing you to be, and to do, and to have. And that wonderful thing is nothing less than what is called *Your Heart's Desire*. Nothing less than that. The most secret, sacred wish that lies deep down at the bottom of your heart, the wonderful thing that you hardly dare to look at, or to think about—the thing that you would rather die than have anyone else know of, because it seems so far beyond anything that you are, or have at the present time, that you fear that you would be cruelly ridiculed if the mere thought of it were known—that is just the very thing that God is wishing you to do or to be for him. And the birth of that marvelous wish in your soul—the dawning of that secret dream—was the Voice

of God himself telling you to arise and come up higher because he had need of you.[1]

It isn't too late to pull your dreams out of the past, to resurrect them from the cemetery deep within. God is thrilled when the odds are so stacked against us we have no choice but to trust in Him. Our God delights in doing the impossible, loves to confound the restraints we place upon ourselves and Him. This same God sent the Israelites marching around a walled city, then at the blast of trumpets knocked over the walls. This same Lord made a whole nation from a child conceived by a century-old couple; the same Savior provided food in the desert and water from a rock. This same God holds our dreams in His heart, longing to see them bear fruit for eternity.

Death of a Dream

Someone may have stolen your dream when it was young and fresh and you were innocent. If someone has damaged the innocence of your dreams,

Anger is natural.

Grief is appropriate.

Healing is mandatory.

Restoration is possible.

Perhaps it isn't another's fault that we haven't reached for our dreams. We dreamt of a career at twenty, missed that and shot for a revised version at thirty; at forty, we bagged a decade of lost dreams. At fifty, we released our freedom to dream and resigned ourselves to a day-by-day existence. We have forgotten to spend our lives on something that outlasts our lives.

Life doesn't always go the way we hoped; there are inevitable disappointments and roadblocks and negative people and problems. We make poor choices, and the consequences seem to choke out any possibilities of furthering our dreams. And so we decide it's safer to keep our feet on the ground and our heart there, too, and bury our desires in the hot sand of doubt and fear.

Fear of a Dream

To avoid the fear of failure and the fear of another's opinion, we stuff our dreams and fritter away our desires on smaller, attainable *things*: a new sweater, a car, a CD, redecorating the living room, an expensive toy. How many shoes can we wear? How much television can we watch? We don't dare to risk the chance of failure, but living with the underlying nausea leaves us always grasping the next placebo. How horrible, though, to echo Thoreau's words, "Oh, God, to reach the point of death only to realize you have never lived." We must not allow fear to snuff out our flickering faith when the winds of the Spirit long to fan that faith into flames.

Susan Jeffers says, "We cannot escape fear. We can only transform it into a companion that accompanies us on all our exciting adventures. . . . Take a risk a day—one small or bold stroke that will make you feel great once you have done it."

Risking a Dream

Dreams become less of a risk and more of an adventurous investment, when we turn to the Author of our highest dreams. For this is the One who told us only to ask and it would be given to us:

> "Now suppose one of you fathers is asked by his son for a fish; he will not give him a snake instead of a fish, will he? Or if he is asked for an egg, he will not give him a scorpion, will he? If you then, being evil, know how to give good gifts to your children, how much more shall your heavenly Father give the Holy Spirit to those who ask Him?" (Luke 11:11–13).

For our dreams are safe in the nail-pierced hands of the One who dreamt of our salvation, the One who provides us with His unlimited power through the Holy Spirit. We are only limited in our asking.

We only fail when we fail to dream.

Share Your Dream

Dreams are least threatening in the dark, secret places of our souls. But they remain there, decaying along with our bodies, until we muster the courage to bring them into the light. Opening the box of my own soul, I placed my dream in the Lord's trustworthy hands and into my husband's loving embrace; but it was hard to trust a dream child to other people. What if they didn't like this baby? What if they thought I'd be a poor mother, inadequate at nursing this dream to full growth?

Part of my dream strategy had to include some accountability to people who affirmed my capabilities. Clearly, I couldn't share a dream baby with someone who believed in child sacrifice! Ultimately, I brought my dream to a circle of friends whom I trusted. They would not encourage an abortion; these women would act as midwives. Here was a safe place but also a challenging one. "What have you written, Jane? How's it going?" they would want to know. And when I signed up for my first writer's conference, they were thrilled. "You will be a woman of letters one day, Jane."

And eventually I brought myself to answer the dreaded stranger-question.

"So what do you do, Jane?"

I never told the whole truth. Wife and mother, yes. Pastor's wife, sometimes. One day, finally, with shaking voice I told the rest: "I am a writer." Immediately, I qualified it. "Well, that is, I write, but I've only sold one article, and it's not in print, and they only paid me $85, and I've had a lot of rejection letters, in fact I won an award for having the most rejections in a roomful of writers, but . . ." Running out of breath and rationalizations and apologies, I finished, "But I am a writer."

Whatever our dream, it is much easier to dream and labor in the birthing room surrounded by people who will breathe and pant with us through the birth of our dream child.

Dream It and Do It!

This is a "free for all." Dreaming has nothing to do with whether our dreams are realistic or manageable. It has everything to do with freeing ourselves from restrictions so we can imagine unhindered. In this creative exercise, we free the Holy Spirit to draw us in the right direction. There is time enough to worry about the how and the when (the next chapter!); now we listen; we tear open our soundproof lives and bring out the music God placed within.

As we dream, the restraints on the chords of our souls fall away. Gently, ever so patiently, the Musician plucks the strings of our hearts, and, if we listen carefully, we will hear a melody forming on the staff of our spirits. And as our mouths form notes never before voiced, a new song emerges, a song of praise to our God. May many be drawn to the Lord as you dream—and sing—a new song. (See Ps. 40:3.)

Quotes for Contemplation ─────────────────

If one advances confidently in the direction of his dreams, and endeavors to live the life which he has imagined, he will meet with a success unexpected in common hours.

—**HENRY DAVID THOREAU**

Press on. Nothing can take the place of persistence. Talent will not; the world is full of unsuccessful people with talent. Genius will not; unrewarded genius is almost a proverb. Education alone will not; the world is full of educated derelicts. Persistence and determination alone are omnipotent.

—**CALVIN COOLIDGE**

What do I mean by loving ourselves properly? I mean first of all, desiring to live, accepting life as a very great gift and a great good, not because of what it gives us, but because of what it enables us to give others.

—**THOMAS MERTON**

Until one is committed, there is hesitance, the chance to draw back. Always ineffectiveness. Concerning all acts of initiative (and creation), there is one elemental truth the ignorance of which kills countless ideas and splendid plans; that the moment one commits oneself, then providence moves too. All sorts of things occur to help one that would never have otherwise occurred. A whole stream of events issues from the decision, raising in one's favor all manner of unforeseen incidents and meetings and material assistance which no man could have dreamed would come his way. Whatever you can do or dream you can begin it. Boldness has genius, power and magic in it. Begin it now.

—**JOHANN WOLFGANG VON GOETHE**

Courage is the capacity to go from failure to failure without losing your enthusiasm.

—**BRITISH PRIME MINISTER WINSTON CHURCHILL**

Sometimes our fears reassure us that we are alive, even as they keep us from really living. . . . You can accept fear as an emotion, even as a fact, but not as a force to hold you back.

—**LES BROWN, LIVE YOUR DREAMS**

Scriptures for Meditation

Lord, all my desire is before Thee;

And my sighing is not hidden from Thee.
                                                        —PSALM 38:9

"For I know the plans that I have for you," declares the Lord, "plans for welfare and not for calamity to give you a future and a hope. Then you will call upon Me and come and pray to Me, and I will listen to you. And you will seek Me and find Me, when you search for Me with all your heart."
                                              —JEREMIAH 29:11–13

*I will instruct you and teach you
in the way which you should go;
I will counsel you with My eye upon you.*
                                                        —PSALM 32:8

"And I say to you, ask, and it shall be given to you; seek, and you shall find, knock, and it shall be opened to you. For everyone who asks, receives; and he who seeks, finds; and to him who knocks, it shall be opened."
                                                  —LUKE 11:9–10

*Therefore the Lord longs to be gracious to you,
And therefore He waits on high to have compassion on you.
For the Lord is a God of justice;
How blessed are all those who long for Him. . . .
    And your ears will hear a word behind you, "This is the way, walk in it, "whenever you turn to the right or to the left."*
                                              —ISAIAH 30:18, 21

Now to Him who is able to do exceeding abundantly beyond all that we ask or think, according to the power that works within us, to Him be the glory in the church and in Christ Jesus to all generations forever and ever. Amen.
                                              —EPHESIANS 3:20–21

I ask him [the Father] to strengthen you by his Spirit . . . that Christ will live in you as you open the door and invite him in. And I ask him that with both feet planted firmly on love, you'll be able to take in with all Christians the extravagant dimensions of Christ's love. Reach out and

*experience the breadth! Test its length! Plumb the depths! Rise to the
heights! Live full lives, full in the fullness of God.*

*God can do anything, you know—far more than you could ever
imagine or guess or request in your wildest dreams! He does it not by
pushing us around but by working within us, his Spirit deeply and gently
within us.*

**—EPHESIANS 3:16–20,
THE MESSAGE**

*Trust in the Lord and do good;
   dwell in the land and enjoy safe pasture.
Delight yourself in the Lord
   and he will give you the desires of your heart.
Commit your way to the Lord;
   trust in him and he will do this:
He will make your righteousness shine like the dawn,
   the justice of your cause like the noonday sun.*

—PSALM 37:3–6, NIV

Journaling

What thoughts, longings, past pains confront you as you contemplate
dreaming of your future? Take some time to journal through your reactions, how your dreams have changed through the years, and where you
land in thinking of dreams today. Where does the Lord enter into the
dreaming process? How do you honestly think He feels about all this
dreaming business?

Prayers of Confession, Praise, Petition

Either in writing, in your heart, or aloud, contemplate the wonders all
around. Let your spirit rise in a song of praise to our marvelous Creator,
who planted not only a world-full of beauty outside but the seeds of
dreams within our hearts. Invite the Holy Spirit to make a clean sweep of
your soul, praise Him for His forgiveness, and then inventory the people
and priorities and problems, placing them in the loving Father's hands.

Moments for Creation

Imagine! All the world was once a dream, a thought, in the mind of
the Trinity until they spoke the world into existence! Today as you walk,

let the Lord's creativity and care wash over you. May your mind and heart fill with praise, and through your praise may you begin to dream.

Silence

As you begin to enter the silence, as you draw near to the very soul of God, invite Him to tune your heart to hear His whisper. Perhaps you might choose a phrase about God, or a favorite name for the Lord, which reminds you of His creative and patient love. You may want to keep a pencil and a blank sheet of paper nearby to record afterward impressions or a word that recurred in your mind or a dream that began to nudge.

Questions for Reflection

1. Before we can dream, we often need to examine ourselves for excess baggage that weighs us down. "Right now, write down all your bad habits and faults and all the mistakes you have made in your life. Did you hurt someone? Did you malign someone? Did you waste an opportunity? Have you written down everything that has nagged and eaten at you over the years? Good. Now take that piece of paper, tear it to shreds and throw it away. Forgive yourself for your faults and your mistakes and move on. The way to your dreams is now clear!"[2]

2. Remember your childhood dreams? What did you long to do or to be when you grew up? Did you voice these dreams to anyone? What did people say in response? Did you have someone who especially encouraged you in your dreams?

3. Did your dreams get snagged on someone else's rough edges? Perhaps you need to grieve the ruins of broken dreams. Take up the shards of your past and place the bits and pieces into the Potter's hand. Give your pain and disappointments to Him and cherish this promise close to your heart:

   The Lord is near to the brokenhearted,
   And saves those who are crushed in spirit. (Psalm 34:18)

4. If you could introduce yourself with any title you wanted, what would it be? Fill in the blanks: I am _____(*name*), and I am a _____ (*dream*). Pretend money, time, and failure are not problems. What would you do? Where would you go? What career would you choose?

5. Do you fritter away your dream on safe, tangible, no-risk things? Does someone in your life belittle your dreams? Does someone with enormous needs and pervasive discontent make you feel you cannot afford to dream? How is the Lord leading you to respond?

6. Find a safe person in whom to confide the secret longings of your heart. Ask him or her to pray for you and to hold you accountable. Then decide to take one risk per day on this new adventure (write it down here), clasp hands with Jesus, and step out on the beginning of a great lifelong adventure!

Hymn of Praise ————————————————

Be Thou My Vision

Be Thou my vision, O Lord of my heart;
Naught be all else to me, save that Thou art.
Thou my best thought, by day or by night,
Waking or sleeping, Thy presence my light.

Be Thou my wisdom, and Thou my true word;
I ever with Thee and Thou with me, Lord;
Thou and Thou only, first in my heart,
Great God of heaven, my treasure Thou art.

Great God of heaven, my victory won,
May I reach heaven's joys, O bright heaven's Sun!

Heart of my own heart, whatever befall,
Still be my vision, O Ruler of all.

—ANCIENT IRISH;
TRANS. BY MARY E. BYRNE;
VERSED BY ELEANOR H. HULL

Alternate Hymn

IN MY HEART THERE RINGS A MELODY

I have a song that Jesus gave me,
It was sent from heaven above;
There never was a sweeter melody,
'Tis a melody of love.

In my heart there rings a melody,
There rings a melody with heaven's harmony;
In my heart there rings a melody,
There rings a melody of love.

I love the Christ who died on Calvary,
For He washed my sins away;
He put within my heart a melody,
And I know it's there to stay.

In my heart there rings a melody,
There rings a melody with heaven's harmony;
In my heart there rings a melody,
There rings a melody of love.

'Twill be my endless theme in glory,
With the angels I will sing;
'Twill be a song with glorious harmony,
When the courts of heaven ring.

In my heart there rings a melody,
There rings a melody with heaven's harmony;
In my heart there rings a melody,
There rings a melody of love.

—ELTON M. ROTH[3]

CHAPTER ELEVEN

Tending the Dream: Gifts and Goals

Priorities must be determined by the goals we set in response to our gifts. Our natural bent is to determine our direction by the needs pressing in upon us; defining priorities based on a needy world defies the way Jesus lived.

Thick, lush carpet muffled my footsteps. A sense of hushed expectancy surrounded me. Light streamed through, softly filtering and centering my busy thoughts.

The redwood forest created a holy atmosphere. Trees towered overhead, reaching boughs up and out in praise; my neck ached from looking at the treetops. Standing at the base of one of these giants, I felt dizzy, like a child leaning against an enormous smokestack, eyes focused on the topmost brick, wondering if the chimney would crash on me.

But the redwoods rarely crash. They are extremely disease and drought resistant. The longevity of the stately trees fascinated me, but intrigued me even more after visiting Mount Lassen, the site of a once-active volcano in Northern California. The redwoods do not grow in that region. There we collected lava rocks and neon green lichen, and while the Midwest melted in 105-degree heat, we threw snowballs at one another. Rich and I added chubby foot-long pinecones from the sugar pine to our treasure store and piled them in the back of our aunt's van, tremendously impressed by such a valuable find. No one I knew had pinecones like these.

I dug in my pocket for a souvenir from the redwood trees. This pinecone was the size of my thumbnail. The giants in California started life as small as a robin's egg?

Unlike the sugar pine, the redwood focuses on longevity. To live long and grow high, it must grow deep. Imagine the root system required to support a tree more than three times as tall as my house, and big enough around for a family to sleep in!

This was a powerful moment for me. The redwood, a leader among trees, wanted to teach me something. It didn't need lots of flashy, centerpiece-sized pinecones to accomplish vital things. The secret was first in the roots, and then in the fruit.

So, too, if we are to become the people God intends, we must focus. To tend the dreams God sows in our hearts, to develop into spiritually effective, mature women, we must focus our lives.

Focus on Gifts

Looking at dreams in the previous chapter prepared us to develop the whispers of God in our souls.

"Now concerning spiritual gifts . . . I do not want you to be unaware . . . there are varieties of gifts, but the same Spirit. And there are varieties of ministries, and the same Lord. And there are varieties of effects, but the same God who works all things in all persons" (1 Cor. 12:1, 4–6). God specially prepared each of us with gifts to use in implementing the dreams He plants in the soil of our hearts.[1]

Amazingly, by narrowing our focus to the use of our gifts, our vision broadens.

Why Gifts?

When Ruthie was a baby, I watched with amazement the discovery process of an infant. The day she noticed her hand, it waved in front of her like a flag from another country. Her jerky movements gradually flowed as she learned to move her fingers to work with her hand, which in turn worked with her mouth as she figured out the connection between fingers, mouth, and food (and blocks, and buttons, and . . .). Each day she coordinated various body parts to work with other body parts. Today, a graceful young lady, all her parts work in unison to get her where she needs to go.

As we learn our individual gifts and where they fit in the bigger scheme of the church, a new work is accomplished. Putting those gifts into practice, developing and exercising them in the local church, the church begins to work like the human body. All parts move in unity to accomplish the task: nurturing, supporting, and encouraging one another in the context of the local church. As the church begins to flesh out the body of Christ, becoming a Christlike presence in this world, others are drawn to Him.

Even with the worldwide implications of using our gifts, God is concerned with our value in His sight. Besides building up the church for Christ's work, there's an added personal benefit.

Added Bonus

Katie entered the huge gym, late and breathless. Not an empty spot appeared. Shrinking into herself, this artistic, intelligent woman in her thirties battled tears. Though sought after for her energetic friendship, a chronic sense of uselessness forced Katie backward. Several friends waved, but they hadn't saved her a seat. In a crowd of people, she felt alone and without value.

But as we begin to develop our own gifts, we grow in self-respect and identity, even when alone in a crowd of acquaintances. As Katie began to focus on her identity in Christ and the unique gifts given her, she found that, whether alone in a crowd or surrounded by friends, her sense of value and purpose brought her confidence. She became less dependent on people needing her, thus freeing herself from the slavery of needing to be needed. Her confidence bloomed golden, like daffodils in a walled garden.

One of the beauties of relationships, whether with a spouse, a child, or a friend, is that by spending time together, we call out one another's gifts. And as others begin to exercise those gifts, our respect for them expands as well, strengthening our relationships. It's a lovely circle of growth.

Identifying our gifts leads us into new growth as we revisit lessons learned in the past.

Back to Boundaries

In the chapter "A New Line Dance" we discussed developing boundaries. Now, tending our dream through gifts and goals, we begin to understand more fully *why* we need to develop boundaries. Boundaries protect our special calling from God to use our gifts for the building up of the body, the church, and for drawing people to Jesus Christ.

My garden taught me one way to reinforce boundaries.

Clip the Suckers

The Summer of the Redwood, our garden back home withered and fried in the heat. The only surviving remnant was a prolific squash plant. This vine grew and grew, covering the garden plot, the fences, and creeping through the alley behind our house. Lots of orange flowers developed, more than I could count, and I looked each morning for squash under the huge plate-sized leaves. I hadn't even *planted* squash seeds; what fun it would be to harvest these squash. The bargain of the year for a bargain hunter.

But I didn't know about suckers, tenacious sprouts that grow quickly and blossom. So many pop out that they sap the life from the main plant. Of all the activity in the garden, not one squash was born. Too late, I learned that I needed to pinch off those suckers so the plant could bear fruit.

How like our lives! As women, we have diverse interests and talents. It's easy to dabble in many things, from crafts to sewing to dollhouses to play groups to gourmet cooking to old movies to antiques to first-edition books to . . . (fill in the blank!)

Think about the great Christian leaders you know. What if Billy Graham hadn't focused on his gifts? What if C. S. Lewis hadn't concentrated on writing? What if Susanna Wesley had focused on parenting but forgotten her mind? With eighteen children, that would be understandable. This woman tutored her children in Hebrew and Greek. More than a hundred denominations claim their origins in her son John; Charles became the most prolific hymn writer of all time. What if John and Charles hadn't focused on their gifts?

And so on it goes. To truly become the people God designed us to be, we must focus. Clip the suckers. My friend Lynn quit making her own health food, stopped teaching cooking classes at the YMCA, gave away her craft items, and began to narrow her interests. Her books and speaking have changed many lives.

We have to ask ourselves: What involvements don't fit with my gifts? What can I eliminate to learn my passion, to identify my gifts, and to infuse my action with purpose?

Thoreau said, "The cost of a thing is the amount of what I call life

which is required to be exchanged for it, immediately or in the long run."
So we ask: How much will this activity or commitment cost me and my
family, emotionally and time-wise? How much energy do I have for this
project, that phone call?

These are good questions, but saying yes to the right involvements is
harder than taking a splinter out of a small child. And saying no . . . well,
what if someone doesn't like me? Or perhaps we think, "They *need* me to
fill this gap."

Yes, But . . .

"Jane, the nominating committee just met, and we'd love to have you
be our Sunday school superintendent. Would you consider the position?"
I groaned at Diane's invitation.

"Diane, I'd love to serve—somewhere else. Maybe an adult Sunday
school class, or an adult forum? Administrating a committee is something
I do poorly. I'm so last minute; I dislike making phone calls; it's hard to
take time to delegate. I'm sorry. I have to say no. Call me about one of the
others, okay?"

A new life motto began to develop from that frightening, "I'm sorry, I
can't." *The Need Does Not Denote the Calling.* Even Jesus, who delighted
to help people, implemented this policy.

Mark 1:29–34 describes The Pastor's Dream: streams of people fill the
road and lane leading to the house. Indeed, "the whole city had gathered
at the door." Dramatic healings, huge ministerial successes, changed lives:
it all happens right here. And then Jesus heads off alone to pray. When
His disciples find Him, they're thrilled to be part of a Prime-Time Event.
"Come on back, Lord, things are happening! The world is at your feet."
But at the pinnacle of success, when scores of needy people need still
more of Him, Jesus says in effect, "Time to go, folks."

Jesus, surrounded by clamoring crowds of needy people, didn't heal
them all, even though He could have. Though He was capable, He didn't
feed every hungry person. He didn't enter every house, He didn't work
twenty-four hours a day preaching and teaching and healing. He did not
let the need determine His calling. He did not allow His agenda to be
determined by others' neediness, or by holes in the program.

No. Jesus' calling and agenda were determined not by people's needs
but by time spent with His Father.

Can we be any less directed?

Regardless of the slot, slot-filling is not faithfulness. God is more interested in our becoming everything He created us to be through the im-

plementation of the unique gifts given us. Saying no to heading a committee frees us to serve in the Sunday school. By declining to lead the
women's ministry, we're free to coordinate hospitality. Saying no, with the
intention of saying yes in the area of our gifts, lines up with God's desire
for our lives. Plus, saying yes to something that doesn't fit us prevents
someone else from saying yes to the very thing they are gifted to do.

So why is it so hard to say yes and no at the proper times?

"The inability to say no arises when we are unsure of who we are and
of what we are supposed to be doing," writes William Willimon. "We say
yes to everything out of fear that we may say no to the thing we truly ought
to be doing."[2]

I said no to Diane's request because I knew myself. I knew my limitations and was beginning to sense my gifts. As we learn who we are, we
begin to see God's agenda unfold.

Wake-Up Call

After beginning to eliminate the "suckers," what's next in forwarding
our dream and living out our gifts? Anne Ortlund says, in *Disciplines of
the Beautiful Woman*, we have to set our goals before we decide where to
set our alarms. What will it take to develop our dream through using our
gifts? We must break down an immeasurable idea such as "I will grow in
evangelism, one of my gifts," into steps. Some steps might include asking
about training in the church, talking with others about evangelism, reading up on Scripture, teaming up with someone similarly gifted. These goals
will keep us on the path.

Steering Straight

Reading back through an old journal, I found a section I wrote at
Christmas when my son, Joshua, was two. "Haven't written a line all week;
company coming tomorrow; Rich out of town." Then I listed everything I
hoped to accomplish given these facts: toddler; single parenting; company; and I could write only during Joshua's nap.

The list contained enough to keep me busy during a forty-hour work
week with no family responsibilities. It's not surprising that I only checked
portions of a couple items off that list.

Be realistic. This is the first element of goal-setting. We gain nothing
believing we can accomplish the work of three women devoting full-time
attention to a project. And we lose by deciding that, given current responsibilities, we can accomplish nothing. Being faithful to work out the

gifts that have been worked into us demands realistic goals. How much time and energy do I have?

Be faithful. This is the second order of the day. As a writer, I try to write some every day, even if it's journaling and a thank-you note, or research/ reading on a subject. This way, I make sure that my gift is being put into service. A composer friend does the same, writing music or working on harmonies or lyrics daily, in between "day job" and family responsibilities.

Be content. As our third task, this means no "Body Envy," no comparing our gifts with others'. "I can't speak like he can." "I can't work one on one with someone like she can." "I can't . . ." Soon we could talk ourselves out of developing those gifts at all. The key word is "develop." We are all in the process of maturing, and some people are naturally further along. We must be content to enter the game at the right time, to grow in our abilities as we practice them. These goals help us to expand the confines of our souls.

Soul-Room

The fogs of the dream began drifting away as I struggled from sleep. Grabbing at the wisps, I replayed the story line in my mind. What had happened? The trip-hammer of my heart told me something significant was transpiring.

I knew the house very well. It was my home. In retrospect I wonder at some of the details, but the certainty remained: in the dream, this was my home, and it was not a new home. I could reach out my hand in the dark of night and know exactly what I would touch. No fumbling, no unfamiliarity.

But what about that door off to the side? This was new. A different place. Someone guided me through the door, and I was astonished to see an entire office set up, complete with chair, desk, books, and typewriter. The room kept going, opening into ever new space, and as I passed through the room, my wonder grew. What a surprise! Here was a gift I hadn't expected.

Awake, I was not surprised that the door opened onto a fully outfitted office. The first time I dreamt this scenario, my heart was whispering, "Write, write." Always other commitments snatched the words, hurling them away into thin air. Fear shushed the whisper: fear of failure, of rejection, of others laughing at me.

Clarity came before I shoved out of bed. The house stood for my soul, one in which I lived happily. But the new room? What about that? It seemed to mean a soul-area I hadn't explored, a place where the invitation stood: come in, live here, try out this chair, use this pen. Explore this room created for you.

The sense of surprise, of a birthday-present-type event, remained throughout the day. Knowing the gift lay there, awaiting my eager unwrapping, filled me with a sense God's love for me.

"Close your eyes and hold out your hands!" my mother loved to say. "For me?" I whispered, delight shining from my face.

"Close your eyes and hold out your hands!" our Father loves to say, knowing that the gifts He places in our outstretched souls will not only light up our faces, they will light up our world.

As you enter the hidden rooms of your soul, the gifts waiting for you there will delight you. Listen! Listen for the voice, echoing through time:

"Well done, good and faithful servant. . . . Enter into the joy of your master" (Matt. 25:21, RSV).

Welcome home.

Quotes for Contemplation

Looking back, I notice at least three things I did to hasten the process of self-understanding and acceptance. First, I chose to consciously cooperate with God's love. Then second, I chose to risk spiritual growth even when it hurt. And third, I determined to discover and use the "gifts" God has given me for the good of others.

. . . I am convinced that the key to long-term self-worth lies in the discovery, not of talents, but rather of spiritual gifts which God has given to every person who has chosen to follow Christ. . . . There's a great difference between talents and gifts. I am certainly pleased that I once developed the talent the Lord gave me, but I'm even more delighted that the spiritual gifts the Lord gives to every believer have been developed in my life also. It is my own theory that while talents may diminish with age, gifts only seem to improve and deepen with the passing of the years. That's very important, and that's why I believe that women in leadership need to work hard at discovering and developing their gifts.

—**GAIL MACDONALD,**
HIGH CALL, HIGH PRIVILEGE

One of the points that struck me . . . was the truth that, under the influence of the gifts, not only the theological, but the infused moral virtues, become immediate avenues of contact with God.

— THOMAS MERTON,
A SEARCH FOR SOLITUDE

Success? I don't know quite what you mean by success. Material success? Worldly success? Personal, emotional success? The people I consider successful are so because of how they handle their responsibilities to other people, how they approach the future, people who have a full sense of the value of their life and what they want to do with it. I call people 'successful' not because they have money, or their business is doing well, but because, as human beings, they have a fully developed sense of being alive and engaged in a lifetime task of collaboration with other human beings—their mothers and fathers, their family, their friends, their loved ones, the friends who are dying, the friends who are being born.

Success? Don't you know it is all about being able to extend love to people? Really. Not in a big, capital-letter sense but in the everyday. Little by little, task by task, gesture by gesture, word by word.

— RALPH FIENNES,
ACTOR (THE ENGLISH PATIENT,
SCHINDLER'S LIST)

As we minister in a way that is consistent with the way God made us, we will find new passion for ministry.

— BILL HYBELS,
THE GREATEST LESSON

The word discipline means "the effort to create some space in which God can act." Discipline means to prevent everything in your life from being filled up. It means somewhere you're not occupied, and you're certainly not preoccupied. It means to create that space in which something can happen that you hadn't planned on or counted on.

— HENRI NOUWEN,
LEADERSHIP JOURNAL

I see now that I spent most of my life doing neither what I ought nor what I liked.

— C. S. LEWIS,
THE SCREWTAPE LETTERS

Scriptures for Meditation ————————————

It's in Christ that we find out who we are and what we are living for. Long before we first heard of Christ and got our hopes up, he had his eye on us, had designs on us for glorious living, part of the overall purpose he is working out in everything and everyone. . . .

That's why, when I heard of the solid trust you have in the Master Jesus and your outpouring of love to all the Christians, I couldn't stop thanking God for you—every time I prayed, I'd think of you and give thanks. But I do more than thank, I ask—ask the God of our Master, Jesus Christ, the God of glory—to make you intelligent and discerning in knowing him personally, your eyes focused and clear, so that you can see exactly what it is he is calling you to do, grasp the immensity of this glorious way of life he has for Christians, oh, the utter extravagance of his work in us who trust him—endless energy, boundless strength!

— **EPHESIANS 1:11–12, 15–19,**
THE MESSAGE

The Lord will fulfill his purpose for me;
your love, O Lord, endures forever—
do not abandon the works of your hands.

— **PSALM 138:8, NIV**

So teach us to number our days,
That we may present to Thee a heart of wisdom.

— **PSALM 90:12**

"How long will you wait before you begin to take possession of the land that the Lord, the God of your fathers, has given you?"

— **JOSHUA 18:3, NIV**

For I am mindful of the sincere faith within you, which first dwelt in your grandmother Lois, and your mother Eunice, and I am sure that it is in you as well. And for this reason I remind you to kindle afresh the gift of God which is in you through the laying on of my hands. For God has not given us a spirit of timidity, but of power and love and discipline.

— **2 TIMOTHY 1:5–7**

And since we have gifts that differ according to the grace given to us, let each exercise them accordingly.

— **ROMANS 12:6**

Journaling

Gifts, goals, passions, dreams. . . . How do you feel about all of these topics? Can you sum it up in one word, one sentence? What Scripture quickened your heart as you read it? What quote touched you? Spend some time reflecting on your reactions.

Prayers of Confession, Praise, Petition ————————

As you confess your sins today, remember the one "gifts" passage that closes with, "but the greatest of these is love" (1 Cor. 13:3). Where have you failed to love, or loved with impure motives? Where has your love demanded repayment? Where have you looked for love when you could have simply looked to the Lord? As your soul is cleansed, imagine the one God endowing each of us with special gifts! What an item for praise! Then, filled with thankfulness for God's gifts to us, share the concerns you have for those you love.

Moments for Creation ————————————————

What a time to bask in God's creation, to let His love reflect from His handiwork! May His benediction rest on you as you spend time with Him.

Silence ————————————————————————

Here you might choose one Scripture portion that resonates within. Read it aloud, then allow the Lord to burn into your heart His message for you within that passage. Focus your thoughts on Him in worship.

Questions for Reflection ————————————————

1. What do you do that energizes you? In what places do you dread serving? Are there committees you absolutely loathe to serve on? Why? What exhausts you in ministry? Where do you see God blessing your work in the church and community? On what do people comment regarding your serving in your local church?

2. Now rephrase the dream that began to evolve from the last chapter, "Nurturing Your Dream." What parallels do you see between your dream and the answers to question 1?

3. What fears arise as you consider looking for your special gifts?

4. Does your local church offer a "Discovering Your Gifts" session or course for Sunday school? If not, you might express an interest in one. For further study, check into some of the resources available for understanding spiritual gifts. Other churches in your community might offer such a session as well.

5. List all the excuses you can think of for NOT finding your gifts and passions, NOT setting boundaries, NOT setting and working some goals to begin to implement those gifts and passions (for example, I'm too tired, too young—or too old! I don't know enough Scripture, I'm too inexperienced . . .). One person asked, "Do you know how old I'll be before I play the piano well enough to play it in church?" The answer: "Exactly the same age you will be if you don't."

6. Now take those excuses and place them before God. Offer them to Him, that He might replace the fear and anxiety behind the excuses with His peace *and* a firm sense of His guidance. "Faithful is He who calls you, and He also will bring it to pass" (1 Thess. 5:24).

7. What is God directing you to do regarding your dreams and goals?

Hymn of Praise —————————————————

Take My Life, and Let It Be

Take my life, and let it be
consecrated, Lord, to Thee.
Take my moments and my days;
let them flow in ceaseless praise.
Take my hands, and let them move
at the impulse of Thy love.
Take my feet, and let them be
swift and beautiful for Thee.

Take my voice, and let me sing
always, only, for my King.
Take my lips, and let them be
filled with messages from Thee.
Take my silver and my gold;
not a mite would I withhold.
Take my intellect, and use
every power as Thou shalt choose.

Take my will, and make it Thine;
it shall be no longer mine.
Take my heart, it is Thine own;
it shall be Thy royal throne.
Take my love, my Lord, I pour
at Thy feet its treasure store.
Take myself, and I will be
ever, only, all for Thee.

—Frances Havergal

CHAPTER TWELVE

Detours in the Journey: Making the Most of Transitions

Transitions are a given on this road called living. Learning to see them not just as stressors but as a means for God to transcend our everydays with His all-encompassing grace will move us on in our journey.

The sun pours over me, an overture bright and promising. I squint in the light, shielding my eyes to peer ahead. The road shimmers in the heat, beckoning me forward. I know I must walk this byway, but I am frightened. Before even stepping out, weariness overtakes me. Can I do this trip? Can I put one foot in front of the other? The route is long and often difficult; dangerous passages as well as peaceful valleys line the way.

I am a transient, always on the ragged edge of starvation. "Who will feed me on this journey?" my anxious soul pleads. The sharp teeth of homesickness forever nibble at the selvages of my spirit. "Where," I beg, "is home?"

The word "journey" fascinates me. *Jour* is the French word for "day."

Implicit in a journey is the daily-ness of the trip, the step-by-step process of traveling. "One day at a time" is a favorite saying of those in recovery groups. For people in transit, who can see only to the next hill or turn in the road, we too must walk our journey one day, indeed, one step, at a time.

Transition. In transit. The word asks, "Where are we going?" "What is the point of our trip?" "Is *how* we travel as important as our destination?"

These questions prick like a burr in our sock as we walk our pilgrim journey. But rather than stop and remove the burr, we limp on. For we are all in transitions of some sort.

Types of Transition

Couples lined the room, all of us in our thirties. Around the circle we learned one another's history: where we've lived, for how long. Rich and I had moved, hoping this would be home for us for many years. Hopping from place to place had lost its appeal, and we yearned for a long-term home and community. Given my mindset, one couple's words surprised me. "We're looking at North Carolina; we'd like to live there." Another couple said, "The Midwest is great, but we have our eye on Oklahoma."

One in six families moves every twelve months, which means that the average family relocates every six years or so. We are a nation in flux, with short, shallow roots. In a mobile society, moving is probably the most high-profile type of transition.

But all transitions involve change. In fact, every line of the stress test in the chapter, "In the Vise: Squeezing the Best Out of Stress" concerns change and transition.

For instance, René left a profession with recognition and monetary rewards for a baby who never stopped crying. René wondered why her own tears were so close to the surface. Sue's children all left home within a week; she spiraled into a two-year depression as she tried to find out "what she wanted to be when she grew up." When Mary changed churches because of logistical problems, Sundays reminded her painfully of her loss. Grethe's declining health meant she could not accompany her friends on their bus outings. With her world now the size of the television screen, her emotional frailty puzzled her.

A Look at Transitions

All About Change

- change in family relationships: birth, death, engagement, marriage, divorce, empty nest, nursing home
- change in health or life stage
- change in social relationships: friends, co-workers, church family, community relationships and involvements
- change in work: job loss, downsizing, job change (whether locale or type of job), promotion or demotion
- change in location: moving, either to a new home in the same area or to a new community

---

Transition has many faces, each face portraying an element of change and risk. As women, we naturally focus on others. We are geared to smooth the way, to meet the needs of those we love. Thus, we may underrate or ignore the tremendous personal cost of transition. A sense of loss accompanies these transitions: loss of security, loss of control, loss of the familiar.

Transition Trauma

Since transition always involves change, this sense of loss must not surprise us. Stages of grief are normal for transition. Michael Smith notes, "Change often produces anger—a word that comes from the Norse *angr*, which means grief."[1] My journals chart my passage through times of transition: excitement, anxiety, fear, depression, anger, grief, acceptance.[2] Research shows that it may take six months for some of these feelings to even appear, and two years for the anguish to abate.

In addition, we may expect too much of ourselves during a time of transition. This common danger can send us plummeting quickly into depression. After our most recent move, my creativity was slow and sluggish in returning. In my covenant group, Elaine said, "Jane, you cannot put down roots and bear fruit at the same time." She was right. After being transplanted, plants go through a time of shock and dormancy, and then begin to develop their roots. External fruit may be slow in coming.

Like a plant, the trauma of transition may render us temporarily dormant. Sometimes the best work we can do during this time is to rest, read, and pray, refilling depleted spirits. Streamlining, plucking unnecessary ob-

ligations, and avoiding new responsibilities are other ways of recovering
from transition and guarding against the dangers of the journey.

Attending to the traumas of transition gives us the resources to deal
with temptation's companions.

Temptations in Transition

One of the temptations during transition is to isolate ourselves. Maintaining life-sustaining relationships defies our tendency to hole up with
our pain. Believing that no one else could understand, we may be tempted
to withdraw during transitions that are highly personal. Communicating
our feelings to those close to us is vital. On our road from here to there,
isolation leaves us easy prey for other temptations.

Like blisters on our heels, transitions can rub us raw, making us long
for the boots we left behind, for the safety of sameness. The Israelites in
the wilderness moaned for leeks and garlic by the Nile. The oppression of
the past may be preferable to the rigors and risks of wilderness travel. We,
too, may be tempted to turn back, to abandon our search for the promised
land because the road is too difficult.

And if we stay in the path, we will likely face another temptation: seiz-
ing the control panels to keep other areas in our lives constant. Feeling
out of control during transition is common. Not wanting any other problems to deal with, I often attempt to regain control by clutching others
too fiercely, demanding perfection of everyone. This stranglehold can
choke our relationships; trying too hard to exert control over husband or
children or co-workers leads to further alienation.

The greatest danger of all, however, may be the loss of perspective.

Don't Forget the Camera, Dear

In the desert sand, all roads begin to look the same. This cactus looks
like the one before it. Where would the Israelites have ended up had not
the fire guided them by night and the cloud by day? They could not see
the end from the beginning. Like most vacationers, the Israelites forgot
to bring their telescopic lens. In the midst of our transitions, we, too, may
forget the appropriate lens. We may view a life event or life stage or life
change separately, an individual event rather than a point on the road. On
our journey, constant companions dog our steps: fear, anxiety, uncertainty.
Fear of change, anxiety for the future, uncertainty of the continuity of our
lives.

With such dismal traveling partners, it's easy to forget that each stage of transition is part of the bigger journey. We congratulate ourselves for taking one day at a time and forget to ask, "Where does this road lead?" It's time to examine the burr in our sock. "What is the point of this trip?" "Is *how* we travel as important as *where* we're going?"

If change is inevitable, why waste energy bucking it? Will we allow change to change us for the better? Or will we dig in our heels, leaving skid marks all the way? Surviving change cannot, must not, be our only goal. Every event is designed to lead us toward God. We must choose growth instead of control, wholeness instead of safety, healing instead of hiding.

Transitions bring out all our insecurities. Change reminds us sharply that we have no home, that life brings no guarantees. Change urges us to consider our own mortality, to remember that endings are inevitable, but that with each ending comes a beginning. Beyond all this, change issues an invitation to trust. When we trust, the real journey begins. When we trust, we plant ourselves in the arms of the One who can take us home.

In this trusting comes the transformation.

Transformed by Transition

Moses mentors us in transition. Time and again he had to choose: Would he listen to his own insecurities? Would he heed the voices of those who mocked and complained and ridiculed? Would he face his past and emerge a leader? Would he listen to God's reassurances: "I will be with you" (Ex. 3:12)?

As Moses shot off his flurry of excuses about why he should *not* lead the Israelites out of Egypt, God returned every volley. Each answer involved the trustworthiness, the presence, and the power of the Sender (Ex. 3–4). Moses chose to let the trip transform him into a mighty leader.

Popular books tell us that transition is the time to find ourselves and our own power and inner wisdom. For me, these intersections have actually been places where I have seen and acknowledged my own emptiness, my lack of wisdom, my utter inability to propel and steer my vehicle another mile.

But God meets me at every turn, every bend, every stop sign in the road. He extends a hand, inviting me to travel at His side. When I accept God as my traveling companion, I invite Him to transform me.

This invitation becomes a transition in itself, a painful one, as the Holy Spirit reveals my own sin-sick heart, my wayward spirit, my desire for con-

---

Pilgrim's Guide to Progress in Transition

Here from the book of Exodus are some principles for growing through times of transition.

1. Listen for God's call. Tune your ear to hear Him. (Ex. 3:4)
2. Remember God's compassion for your suffering, oppression, and affliction. (Ex. 3:7, 9)
3. Look for God on the way! Take time to "turn aside and see. . . ." (Ex. 3:3)
4. Let God feed you in the wilderness (manna). (Ex. 16:4)
5. Follow the Leader—let Him steer (trust). (Ex. 3:12)
6. Look for companions on the journey (Aaron). (Ex. 4:14–15)
7. Reflect. Moses had to return to the land of his pain and shame in order to become the man God intended. We may need to do the same.
8. Talk about your feelings and anxieties. Moses certainly did! (Ex. 3:11; 4:1, 10, 13)
9. Let God change you. Who you are becoming is as important as where you're going. It's a long journey (forty years for Moses)!
10. Worship. "This shall be the sign . . . you shall worship God at this mountain." (Ex. 3:12)

---

trol and self-sufficiency. Transition becomes more than an intersection; it is also a merge. Even when the road doesn't lead where we thought we were going.

The Invitation

"But the invitation said, '. . . a good and spacious land, a land flowing with milk and honey,' " we wail. "It didn't mention detours, disappointments, and dangers along the way!"

Transitions involve pain, loss, forgiveness, and sometimes a realignment of our dreams. There are bends and turns in the road that we would not choose. But we still have a choice: to bear it on our own or to grow from the journey by turning to God.

With God as our travel agent and tour guide, we book ourselves on a journey with a twofold destination. When we fall into step with Jesus, we take seriously His desire that we be transformed by the journey, regardless of the perils and surprises and ruts in the road. Paul says it well:

We exult in hope of the glory of God. And not only this, but we also exult in our tribulations, knowing that tribulation brings about perseverance; and perseverance, proven character; and proven character, hope; and hope does not disappoint, because the love of God has been poured out within our hearts through the Holy Spirit who was given to us. (Rom. 5:2–5)

We know that God causes all things to work together for good to those who love God, to those who are called according to His purpose . . . to become conformed to the image of His Son. (Rom. 8:28–29)

How amazing that God takes the inevitable transitions in our lives and grants us the opportunity to be changed by them into the very likeness of His precious Son!

But our journey doesn't end here with this transformation. No, God's travel plans include involving others in the very trip we have just taken. He desires that we lead others to the Source of comfort as well.

Thanks be to God, who always leads us in His triumph in Christ, and manifests through us the sweet aroma of the knowledge of Him in every place. (2 Cor. 2:14)

Blessed be the God . . . of all comfort, who comforts us in our affliction so that we may be able to comfort those who are any in affliction with the comfort with which we ourselves are comforted by God. (2 Cor. 1:3–4)

When we are transformed by change, our lives, our actions, and our attitudes invite others to join us. Dale Hanson Bourke writes, "Because we are changed, we are then able to change the world. And suddenly, change begins to happen, not only *in* us, but also *because* of us. And that is the greatest miracle of all."[3]

God didn't promise us an easy journey, but He has promised us His presence, His power, and His purpose as we travel. He knows the trip is long, that we are feeble and tire easily. His presence with us is His final gift.

Grace Will Lead Us Home

"Mom, do you have a headache? You look tired, or sad." Ruthie sits next to me in the pew, concern pinching her face.

I seize on *tired*, but the truth is, it's still a long journey home, a painful trip, full of weary hikes and danger. I am far from being transformed by the journey.

Suddenly, the choir bursts into a new arrangement of their closing anthem. The Spirit pulses as they sing, "'Tis grace hath brought me safe thus far, and grace will lead me home."

Tears sting my eyes. And I know God's words to me: "*Grace* will go with you on this journey. You are not alone. And this place of transition is blessed by Me."

I feel God's presence in this place of in between. Even as I shield my eyes from the sun, I know that en route, the God of transitions accompanies me, guiding my own steps, protecting me. He hems me in behind and before, yet stays by my side.

A realization stuns me. Here the One in whom I live and move and have my being is not only the end of my journey but also the means of my journey.

If this is a desert for you, if this has felt like a long, gritty, endless road to nowhere, if you are parched and squint-eyed from finding your way,

Relax.

Let God find you. Listen for His voice. Turn aside and see the bush that burns but is not consumed. You will find the journey easier when you travel with a Companion.

And—take off your shoes. You are on holy ground. May God bless you as He both transforms you and transports you on your journey.

His grace will lead you home.

Quotes for Contemplation ─────────────────────

Don't ever believe that you are going to be peaceful—life is not like that. When you are changing all the time, you've got to keep adjusting to change, which means that you are going to be constantly facing new obstacles. That's the joy of living. And once you are involved in the process of becoming, there is no stopping. You're doomed! You're gone! But what a fantastic journey!

—LEO BUSCALGIA,
LIVING, LOVING, AND LEARNING

Change happens. That it happens to us is a surprise only at the first great disruption. But that it happens in *us is a mystery more profound*

than birth or death or life itself. Change happens in us not because we will it, but because we are humiliated by how undeserving we are. It happens most often through the clarifying vacuum of tragedy, but it also happens when the good times are not as good as we imagined they would be. Change happens when we open our eyes to the brutality and unfairness and incongruity of life, and we begin to feel the pain of those we don't even know and never cared about.

—**DALE HANSON BOURKE,**
TURN TOWARD THE WIND:
EMBRACING CHANGE IN YOUR LIFE

Maybe death exists as a deadline that forces the issues, so that you have to learn what there is to learn—which is how to enjoy your life— before you die.

—**ANNE LAMOTT,**
HARD LAUGHTER

Worrying is carrying tomorrow's load with today's strength—carrying two days at once. It is moving into tomorrow ahead of time. Worry does not empty tomorrow of its sorrow, it empties today of its strength.

—**CORRIE TEN BOOM,**
HE CARES, HE COMFORTS

It seems as if the Lord has chosen the most unpromising places in which to reveal Himself in might and power, and to encourage us to go forward.

—**GEORGE GRENFELL, AS**
QUOTED IN JOURNAL FOR PILGRIMS

God's call to me, His child, is not to safeness but always to something more—always upward, higher, further along. To by-pass the call is to settle for mediocrity, complacency, and dormancy. And should I choose not to risk, I will more than likely wake up some morning with the haunting question on my mind, "Could God have had something more for me, if only I had dared to trust?"

—**RUTH SENTER,**
BEYOND SAFE PLACES

If you praise the Lord through a minor hardship or a major trial, you are offering a sacrifice of praise. Such a sacrifice costs you plenty—your pride, your anger, your human logic, and the luxury of your complaining tongue. A sacrifice of praise costs you your will, your resentment, and even your desire to have your own way in a situation. And for whose sake do we give up these things? We do so for the sake of Christ and for His glory.

Whether it's a financial crunch, a sudden illness, or a personal defeat, if you fix your heart on praise to God, then you have offered a sacrifice. If you've ever cried during those heartbreaking difficulties, "Lord, I will hope in You and praise You more and more," then you know you have offered words which have cost you plenty. Praise in those circumstances is painful. Nevertheless, it is logical, even if our logic argues that God has no idea what He's doing.

—**JONI EARECKSON TADA,**
A QUIET PLACE IN A CRAZY WORLD

Scriptures for Meditation

"Behold, I will do something new,
Now it will spring forth!
Will you not be aware of it?
I will even make a roadway in the wilderness,
Rivers in the desert."

—**ISAIAH 43:19**

God is our refuge and strength,
A very present help in trouble.
Therefore we will not fear,
though the earth should change,
And though the mountains slip into the heart of the sea;
Though its waters roar and foam,
Though the mountains quake at its swelling pride.
There is a river whose streams make glad the city of God,
The holy dwelling places of the Most High.
God is in the midst of her, she will not be moved;
God will help her when morning dawns. . . .
"Cease striving and know that I am God;
I will be exalted among the nations,
I will be exalted in the earth."
The Lord of hosts is with us;
The God of Jacob is our stronghold.

—**PSALM 46:1–5, 10–11**

Though I walk in the midst of trouble,
Thou wilt revive me;
Thou wilt stretch forth Thy hand
against the wrath of my enemies,
And Thy right hand will save me.
The Lord will accomplish what concerns me;
Thy lovingkindness, O Lord, is everlasting;
Do not forsake the works of Thy hands.

—**Psalm 138:7–8**

Though the fig tree should not blossom,
And there be no fruit on the vines,
Though the yield of the olive should fail,
And the fields produce no food,
Though the flock should be cut off from the fold,
And there be no cattle in the stalls,
Yet I will exult in the Lord,
I will rejoice in the God of my salvation.
The Lord God is my strength,
And He has made my feet like hinds' feet,
And makes me walk on my high places.

—**Habakkuk 3:17–19**

Where can I go from Thy Spirit?
Or where can I flee from Thy presence?
If I ascend to heaven, Thou art there;
If I make my bed in Sheol, behold, Thou art there.
If I take the wings of the dawn,
If I dwell in the remotest part of the sea,
Even there Thy hand will lead me,
And Thy right hand will lay hold of me.
If I say, "Surely the darkness will overwhelm me,
And the light around me will be night,"
Even the darkness is not dark to Thee,
And the night is as bright as the day.
Darkness and light are alike to Thee.

—**Psalm 139:7–12**

Journaling

Psalm 147:2–3 tells us the Lord gathers the exiles of Jerusalem; He heals the brokenhearted and binds up their wounds. God is the Lord of transitions, the Blesser of change, always beckoning us to take His hand for the journey, the day-by-day walking. Write about your journey, the transition you are in right now. Explore your feelings about this time in your life.

Prayers of Confession, Praise, Petition

Empty all the pent-up feelings you have into God's lap. Invite Him to highlight all sin and confess that to Him. As you turn, free and forgiven, praise Him for this miracle, and then entrust your concerns into His capable hands.

Moments for Creation

Sit on the deck, take a hike, stroll a country road. Breathe deeply in the presence of God; let His creation soothe and comfort you as a reminder of the Lord's great love for *you* personally. Invite Him to reveal himself to you as He chooses.

Silence

"To experience the love of God is the longing of the spiritual person. This is our goal in contemplation: to rest in the presence of that love. When we know we are loved by God, we are empowered by the joy which expresses itself in deep praise."[4]

Take time now to simply rest in the presence of God's deep and abiding love.

Questions for Reflection

1. How do you respond to change in your life? Do you embrace it, long for it? Are you always looking for something new? What does the Holy Spirit reveal about your restlessness? Do you dread change, drag against it like a dropped anchor on a sailboat in a stiff breeze? Why? What do you dislike about change, about transition? What do you fear?

2. List the transitions you've experienced in your life. If you like, create a time line, plotting transitions along the way. Note the peaks and valleys. How did you respond to various points on your life graph? Does a pattern emerge? How did your mother and/or father react to change? Are there similarities? Can you invite God to show you the good side of a painful transition?

3. What bends and turns in the road would you not have chosen? What heartaches and disappointments did you experience through them? Share your pain now, allowing the Comforter to hold you in your grief.

4. Where have you fought against transitions? What have you learned about yourself from transitions? How can you book your flight with God, letting Him transport you? What are God's goals for your journey?

Hymn of Praise

GUIDE ME, O THOU GREAT JEHOVAH

Guide me, O Thou great Jehovah,
Pilgrim through this barren land.
I am weak, but Thou art mighty;
Hold me with Thy powerful hand.
Bread of heaven, Bread of heaven,
Feed me till I want no more;
Feed me till I want no more.

Open now the crystal fountain,
Whence the healing stream doth flow;
Let the fire and cloudy pillar
Lead me all my journey through.
Strong Deliverer, strong Deliverer,
Be Thou still my strength and shield;
Be Thou still my strength and shield.

When I tread the verge of Jordan,
Bid my anxious fears subside;
Death of death and hell's destruction,
Land me safe on Canaan's side.
Songs of praises, songs of praises,
I will ever give to Thee;
I will ever give to Thee.

—WILLIAM WILLIAMS;
STANZA ONE TRANS. BY
PETER WILLIAMS

Alternate Hymn

COME, THOU FOUNT OF EVERY BLESSING

Come, Thou Fount of every blessing,
Tune my heart to sing Thy grace;
Streams of mercy, never ceasing,
Call for songs of loudest praise.
Teach me some melodious sonnet,
Sung by flaming tongues above.
Praise the mount! I'm fixed upon it,
Mount of Thy redeeming love.

Here I'll raise mine Ebenezer;
Hither by Thy help I'm come;
And I hope, by Thy good pleasure,
Safely to arrive at home.
Jesus sought me when a stranger,
Wandering from the fold of God;
He, to rescue me from danger,
Interposed His precious blood.

O to grace how great a debtor
Daily I'm constrained to be!
Let Thy goodness, like a fetter,
Bind my wandering heart to Thee.
Prone to wander, Lord, I feel it,
Prone to leave the God I love;
Here's my heart, O take and seal it,
Seal it for Thy courts above.

—ROBERT ROBINSON

Appendix

Where to Look for Quiet Places

Retreat Directories

Sanctuaries: The Northeast and *Sanctuaries: The West Coast and Southwest* by Marcia and Jack Kelly (Crown Publishers). Includes detailed descriptions (with prices) of hundreds of lodgings in monasteries, abbeys, and retreat centers.

Director of Retreat Ministry Centers. An annual listing of hundreds of Christian (primarily Catholic) retreat centers in the United States and Canada. Available for $25 from Retreats International, Box 1067, Notre Dame, IN 46556. 219–631–5320.

NARDA Directory. An ecumenical listing, with brief descriptions of more than two dozen Christian (primarily Protestant) retreat centers, published by the North American Retreat Directors Association. Send $3 to NARDA, P.O. Box 465, Cornwall, NY 12518.

Communities Directory (published by the Fellowship for Intentional Communities). Includes information on communities that offer retreats. Send $19 to FIC Directory, c/o Twin Oaks, Route 4, Box 169, Louisa, VA 23093. 703–894–5126.

In addition:

- Check your local phone book for seminaries, monasteries, or convents nearby. If these don't have rooms available, ask for references.
- Libraries, a friend's home (the friend must not be there!), or a church offer other Quiet Place possibilities.

What to Bring to Your Quiet Place

1. A Bible, journal, and possibly a hymnal are the bare bones for a retreat. You might include favorite meditational reading material.

2. For inspirational music, bring along your favorites, plus a CD or cassette player. Also check out the companion album to *Quiet Places* described on page 181.

3. Food. Check to see if meals are provided at your retreat location. Some offer meals at no extra (or a minimum) charge; others have cooking facilities, in which case you will need to bring food and beverages.

4. A blanket, a pillow, and an alarm clock to chase away the drowsies. (Don't worry if you are tired and need a nap; retreats can be exhausting. Remember, sleep is spiritual!)

5. Shoes. Include comfortable shoes for an enjoyable time outside, along with appropriate outerwear. (Plan for rain and then be pleasantly surprised when the sun shines.) Insect repellent, sunscreen, and a blanket for outdoor use may be welcome additions.

6. Reasonable expectations for your day. Sometimes the mountain does not smoke, and the bush does not burn. But the time spent simply resting in God's loving presence will restore your soul.

Bring *Quiet Places* Closer to Home

If your church or women's ministries is interested in considering the author as a speaker for a women's conference, retreat, or banquet, please contact:

Jane Rubietta
54 S. Whitney Street
Grayslake, Illinois 60030

Music Companion Resource Also Available!

A key Scripture for each chapter of *QUIET PLACES the book* has been selected and given an original, artistic musical rendition on *QUIET PLACES the album*. This new compact disc recording (or cassette) will guide and enrich your spiritual retreat and help you memorize Scripture.

The Reverend Rich Rubietta and friends have written and recorded twelve captivating and inspiring songs that you and your family will find easy to sing and remember. Rev. Rubietta has a music degree from Northwestern University in Evanston, Illinois, and an M.Div. from Trinity Evangelical Divinity School in Deerfield, Illinois.

QUIET PLACES the album is destined to become a devotional classic!

Available at the address above:

Compact Disc: $10.00
Cassette: $8.00
Postage: $2.00

If you wish to purchase *Quiet Places* the book ($10.00) and the CD or cassette as a package, please include total of items plus $4.00 postage.

Works Cited

The publisher gratefully acknowledges permission to reproduce material from the following sources. While every effort has been made to secure permission, we may have failed in a few cases to trace or contact the copyright holder. We apologize for any inadvertent oversight or error.

American Medical Association, 515 N. State Street, Chicago, IL 60610.

Benson, Bob. *Come Share the Being.* Grand Rapids, Mich.: Impact Books/ Zondervan, 1974.

Bourke, Dale Hanson. *Turn Toward the Wind: Embracing Change in Your Life.* Grand Rapids, Mich.: Zondervan, 1995. Used by permission.

Brown, Les. *Live Your Dreams.* New York: William Morrow & Co., Inc., 1992.

Buscalgia, Leo. *Living, Loving, Learning.* New York: Fawcett Books, 1990.

Chapman, Annie, Luci Shaw, and Florence Littauer. *Can I Control My Changing Emotions?* Minneapolis: Bethany House Publishers, 1994.

Cloud, Dr. Henry, and Dr. John Townsend. *Boundaries: When to Say YES, When to Say No, to Take Control of Your Life.* Grand Rapids, Mich.: Zondervan, 1992.

Fox, Emmet. *Your Heart's Desire.* Pamphlet #6. Marina Del Rey, Calif.: DeVorss & Co., 1961.

Glasser, William. *Reality Therapy: A New Approach to Psychiatry.* New York: Harper & Row, 1965.

Gire, Ken. *Incredible Moments With the Savior.* Grand Rapids, Mich.: Zondervan, 1990. Used by permission.

Gordon, Arthur. *Daily Guideposts 1995.* Carmel, N.Y.: Guideposts, 1994.

Hemfelt, Dr. Robert, and Paul Warren. *Kids Who Carry Our Pain.* Nashville: Thomas Nelson, 1990.

Hemfelt, Dr. Robert, and Drs. Frank Minirth and Paul Meier. *We Are Driven: The Compulsive Behavior America Applauds.* Nashville: Thomas Nelson, 1991.

Herklots, Rosamond E. "Forgive Our Sins As We Forgive." *The United Methodist Hymnal.* London: Oxford University Press, 1989.

Houk, Margaret. *Lighten Up and Enjoy Life More: Everyday Ways to De-stress Your Lifestyle.* Valley Forge, Penn.: Judson Press, 1996. Used by permission. 1–800–458–3766.

Howatch, Susan. *Glittering Images.* New York: Alfred A. Knopf, Inc., 1987.

Hybels, Bill, ed. by Bill and Vonnette Bright. *The Greatest Lesson Ever Learned.* Nashville: Thomas Nelson, 1993.

The Interpreter's Bible. vol. 7. Nashville: Abingdon, n.d.

Jensen, Margaret. *Lena.* Eugene, Ore.: Harvest House, 1996. Used by permission.

Kadlecek, Jo. "An Authentic Friendship: An interview with Madeleine L'Engle and Luci Shaw." *Virtue,* Jan/Feb 1997.

Lamott, Anne. *Hard Laughter.* New York: Viking Press, 1980.

Landorf, Joyce. *The High Cost of Growing.* New York: Bantam Books, 1979.

Larsen, Earnie, and Carol Larsen Hegarty. *Days of Healing, Days of Joy: Daily Meditations for Adult Children.* San Francisco: Hazelden Foundation/HarperSan Francisco, 1987.

Lee, Susan. *The Dancer.* Grand Rapids, Mich.: Baker Book House, 1991.

Lerner, Harriet Goldhor, Ph.D. *The Dance of Anger.* New York: Harper & Row, 1985.

———. *The Dance of Intimacy.* New York: HarperCollins, 1989.

Lewis, C. S. *A Grief Observed.* New York: Bantam Books, 1961.

———. *The Screwtape Letters.* Grand Rapids, Mich.: Fleming H. Revell, 1979.

Lucado, Max. *No Wonder They Call Him the Savior.* Sisters, Ore.: Multnomah Books, Questar Publishers, 1986.

MacDonald, Gail. *High Call, High Privilege.* Wheaton, Ill.: Tyndale House, 1981.

MacDonald, George. *Creation in Christ.* Wheaton, Ill.: Harold Shaw Publishers, 1976.

MacDonald, Gordon and Gail. *If Those Who Reach Could Touch.* Chicago: Moody Press, 1984. Used by permission. Quoting from James J. Lynch. *The Broken Heart: The Medical Consequences of Loneliness.* New York: Basic Books, 1979.

Mains, Karen. *Karen Karen.* Wheaton, Ill.: Tyndale House, 1979. Reprinted with permission.

———. *Key to a Loving Heart.* Elgin, Ill.: Chariot Family Publishers, 1988. Reprinted with permission.

Merton, Thomas. *A Search for Solitude: The Journals of Thomas Merton, vol. 3, 1952–1960.* New York: The Merton Legacy Trust/ Harper-Collins, 1996 (Copyright ©1996 by the Merton Legacy Trust).

Miller, Alice. *Prisoners of Childhood: The Drama of the Gifted Child and the Search for the True Self.* New York: Basic Books, Inc., 1981.

Neufeld, Elsie. *Dancing in the Dark.* Waterloo, Ontario: Herald Press, 1990.

Nouwen, Henri. *The Inner Voice of Love.* New York: Doubleday, 1996.

———. "Moving From Solitude to Community to Ministry." *Leadership Journal*, Spring 1995.

———. *The Way of the Heart.* San Francisco: HarperSan Francisco, 1981.

———. *The Wounded Healer.* New York: Doubleday, 1994.

Olsen, Kathy. *Silent Pain.* Colorado Springs: NavPress, 1992.

O'Neil, Mike S., and Charles E. Newbold. *Boundary Power: How I Treat You, How I Let You Treat Me, How I Treat Myself.* Nashville: Sonlight Publishing, Inc., 1994.

Oswald, Roy M. *Clergy Self-Care: Finding a Balance for Effective Ministry.* Used with permission from The Alban Institute, Inc., 7315 Wisconsin Ave., Suite 1250W, Bethesda, MD 20814–3211. Copyright 1991.

Oswald, Roy M., and Otto Kroeger. *Who Ministers to Ministers? A Study of Support Systems for Clergy and Spouses.* Used with permission from The Alban Institute, Inc., 7315 Wisconsin Ave., Suite 1250W, Bethesda, MD 20814–3211. Copyright 1987.

Peace, Richard. *Contemplative Bible Reading: Experiencing God Through Scripture.* Colorado Springs: NavPress, 1996. Used by permission. 1–800–366–7788.

Rader, Dotson. "Success? What About Happiness?" An interview with Ralph Fiennes. *Parade Magazine*, March 9, 1997. Reprinted with permission.

Rubietta, Jane A. "Am I My Sister's Gatekeeper?" *The Lookout*, Nov. 6, 1994. Taken from "How to Do Right When a Friend Does Wrong." *PLUS: The Magazine of Positive Thinking*, vol. 46, no. 6, pt. 3, July/ Aug 1995.

Rubin, Lillian B. *Just Friends: The Role of Friendship in our Lives.* New York: Harper & Row, 1985.

Schuller, Robert. *Self-Esteem: The New Reformation.* Dallas: Word, Inc., 1982. Reprinted with permission.

Senter, Ruth. *Beyond Safe Places*. Wheaton, Ill.: Harold Shaw Publishers, 1992.

Smith, Michael. "Pastors Under Fire: A Personal Report." *The Christian Century*, February 23, 1994.

Swenson, Richard A., M.D. *Margin: Restoring Emotional, Physical, Financial, and Time Reserves to Overloaded Lives*. Colorado Springs: NavPress, 1992. Used by permission. 1–800–366–7788.

Tada, Joni Eareckson. *A Quiet Place in a Crazy World*. Sisters, Ore.: Questar Publishers, 1993.

Ten Boom, Corrie. *He Cares, He Comforts*. Grand Rapids, Mich.: Fleming H. Revell, 1977.

Townsend, John, M.D. *Hiding From Love: How to Change the Withdrawal Patterns That Isolate and Imprison You*. Colorado Springs: NavPress, 1991. Used by permission. 1–800–366–7788.

Wangerin, Walt. *As for Me and My House*. Nashville: Thomas Nelson Publishers, 1990.

Williams, Gordon. "Flaming Out on the Job." *Modern Maturity*, Oct/Nov 1991.

Willimon, William. *Clergy and Laity Burnout*. Nashville: Abingdon Press, 1989.

Books to Read in Your Quiet Places

Austin, Lynn N. *The Lord Is My Strength*. Kansas City, Mo.: Beacon Hill Press, 1995.

Allender, Dr. Dan B., and Dr. Tremper Longman III. *The Cry of the Soul: How Our Emotions Reveal Our Deepest Questions About God*. Colorado Springs: NavPress, 1994.

Barnes, M. Craig. *When God Interrupts: Finding New Life Through Unwanted Change*. Downers Grove, Ill.: InterVarsity Press, 1996.

Beattie, Melody. *The Lessons of Love*. San Francisco: HarperSan Francisco, 1994.

Bradshaw, John. *Healing the Shame That Binds You*. Pompano Beach, Fla.: Health Communications, Inc., 1987.

Cameron, Julia. *The Artist's Way*. New York: G.P. Putnam's Sons, 1992.

Coyle, Neva. *Answering God's Call to Quiet*. Minneapolis: Bethany House Publishers, 1997.

———. *Making Sense of Pain and Struggle*. Minneapolis: Bethany House, 1992.

Dillard, Annie. *Pilgrim at Tinker Creek*. New York: HarperPerennial, 1974.

Fleming, Jean. *The Homesick Heart*. Colorado Springs: NavPress, 1995.

Foster, Richard J. *Celebration of Discipline: The Path to Spiritual Growth*. New York: Harper & Row, 1978.

———. *Prayer: Finding the Heart's True Home*. San Francisco: HarperSan Francisco, 1992.

Hall, Thelma. *Too Deep for Words*. New York: Paulist Press, 1988.

Hendricks, Harville. *Getting the Love You Want*. New York: HarperPerennial, 1988.

Keller, Phillip. *A Shepherd Looks at Psalm 23.* New York: Harper-Paperbacks, 1970.

Kent, Carol. *Secret Passions of the Christian Woman.* Colorado Springs: NavPress, 1991.

———. *Tame Your Fears.* Colorado Springs: NavPress, 1993.

L'Engle, Madeleine. *A Circle of Quiet.* New York: Harper & Row, 1972.

Lindbergh, Anne Morrow. *Gift From the Sea.* New York: Pantheon Books, 1955.

Mains, Karen Burton. *Lonely No More.* Dallas: Word Publishing, 1993.

O'Neil, Mike S., and Charles E. Newbold. *Boundary Power: How I Treat You, How I Let You Treat Me, How I Treat Myself.* Nashville: Sonlight Publishing, Inc., 1994.

Parker, Dr. William R., and Elaine St. Johns. *Prayer Can Change Your Life.* Carmel, N.Y.: Guideposts, 1993.

Peace, Richard. *Contemplative Bible Reading: Experiencing God Through Scripture.* Colorado Springs: NavPress, 1996.

———. *Spiritual Journaling: Recording Your Journey Toward God.* Colorado Springs: NavPress, 1995.

Rhodes, Tricia McCary. *The Soul at Rest: A Journey Into Contemplative Prayer.* Minneapolis: Bethany House Publishers, 1996.

Rosellini, Gayle, and Mark Worden. *Of Course You're Angry: A Family Guide to Dealing With the Emotions of Chemical Dependence.* Minneapolis: Hazelden Books, 1986.

Seamands, David A. *Healing for Damaged Emotions.* Wheaton, Ill.: Victor Books, 1981.

———. *Healing of Memories.* Wheaton, Ill.: Victor Books, 1985.

———. *Putting Away Childish Things.* Wheaton, Ill.: Victor Books, 1993.

Stoop, Dr. David, and Dr. James Masteller. *Forgiving Our Parents, Forgiving Ourselves: Healing Adult Children of Dysfunctional Families.* Ann Arbor, Mich.: Servant Publications, 1991.

Woititz, Janet Geringer, Ed.D. *Struggle for . . . Intimacy.* Pompano Beach, Fla.: Health Communications, Inc., 1985.

Yancey, Philip. *Where Is God When It Hurts?* Grand Rapids, Mich.: Zondervan, 1977.

Endnotes

Introduction

1. *The Interpreter's Bible*, vol. 7, (Nashville: Abingdon), 443.

Chapter 2

1. From a talk delivered in Elmhurst, Illinois, 1983.

Chapter 3

1. Mike S. O'Neil and Charles E. Newbold, *Boundary Power: How I Treat You, How I Let You Treat Me, How I Treat Myself* (Nashville: Sonlight Publishing, Inc., 1994), 5.
2. Dr. John Townsend, *Hiding From Love: How to Change the Withdrawal Patterns That Isolate and Imprison You* (Colorado Springs: NavPress, 1991), 77.
3. Drs. Henry Cloud and John Townsend, *Boundaries: When to Say YES, When to Say NO, to Take Control of Your Life* (Grand Rapids, Mich.: Zondervan, 1992), 151.

Chapter 4

1. Elsie Neufeld, *Dancing in the Dark* (Waterloo, Ontario: Herald Press, 1990), 82.
2. C. S. Lewis, *A Grief Observed* (New York: Bantam Books, 1961), 10.
3. Neufeld, 127.
4. Susan Howatch, *Glittering Images* (New York: Alfred A. Knopf, 1987), 188.

Chapter 5

1. Susan Lee, *The Dancer* (Grand Rapids, Mich.: Baker Book House, 1991), 54.
2. Kathy Olsen, *Silent Pain* (Colorado Springs: NavPress, 1992), 17.
3. From *The United Methodist Hymnal* (1989), 390.

Chapter 7

1. Roy M. Oswald and Otto Kroeger, *Who Ministers to Ministers? A Study of Support Systems for Clergy and Spouses* (Washington, D.C.: The Alban Institute, 1987), 6.
2. American Medical Association, 515 N. State Street, Chicago, IL 60610.
3. Gordon Williams, "Flaming Out on the Job," *Modern Maturity* (Oct/Nov 1991): 26–27.

Chapter 8

1. Dr. Lillian B. Rubin, *Just Friends: The Role of Friendship in Our Lives* (New York: Harper & Row, 1985).
2. Portions of these pages first appeared in "Am I My Sister's Gatekeeper?" *The Lookout* (November 6, 1994): 8, 14; and in "How to Do Right When a Friend Does Wrong," *PLUS: The Magazine of Positive Thinking* (July/Aug 1995): Vol. 46, No. 6, Part III, 26–35. Copyright Jane A. Rubietta.
3. Harriet Goldhor Lerner, Ph.D., *The Dance of Intimacy* (New York: HarperCollins, 1989), 3.
4. Roy M. Oswald, *Clergy Self-Care: Finding a Balance for Effective Ministry* (Washington, D.C.: The Alban Institute, 1991), 130.
5. Gordon and Gail MacDonald, *If Those Who Reach Could Touch* (Chicago: Moody Press, 1984), 4; quoting from James J. Lynch, *The Broken Heart: The Medical Consequences of Loneliness* (New York: Basic Books, 1979).

Chapter 10

1. Emmet Fox, *Your Heart's Desire*, Pamphlet #6 (Marina Del Rey, Calif.: DeVorss and Co., 1961).

2. Les Brown, *Live Your Dreams* (New York: William Morrow & Co., Inc., 1992), 85.
3. Hope Publishing Co., 1924; Renewal 1951.

Chapter 11

1. Various Scriptures emphasize the presence, types, and use of gifts. For further study, you might examine 1 Corinthians 12; Romans 12:3–16; Ephesians 4:11. In addition, many fine resources are available to assist us in determining which gifts have been given to each of us.
2. William Willimon, *Clergy and Laity Burnout* (Nashville: Abingdon Press, 1989), 63.

Chapter 12

1. Michael Smith, "Pastors Under Fire: A Personal Report," *The Christian Century* (February 23, 1994): 197.
2. If grief best describes your feelings during this time of transition, you may want to revisit the chapter "Learning From Our Losses."
3. Dale Hanson Bourke, *Turn Toward the Wind: Embracing Change in Your Life* (Grand Rapids, Mich.: Zondervan, 1995), 107.
4. Richard Peace, *Contemplative Bible Reading: Experiencing God Through Scripture* (Colorado Springs: NavPress, 1996), 19.

Thank you for selecting a book from
BETHANY HOUSE PUBLISHERS

Bethany House Publishers is a ministry of Bethany Fellowship International, a nondenominational, nonprofit organization committed to spreading the Good News of Jesus Christ around the world through evangelism, church planting, literature distribution, and care for those in need. Missionary training is offered through Bethany College of Missions.

Bethany Fellowship International is a member of the National Association of Evangelicals and subscribes to its statement of faith. If you would like further information, please contact:

Bethany Fellowship International
6820 Auto Club Road
Minneapolis, MN 55438 USA